Praise for EDUCATING ESMÉ

"The imagination and irreverent wit [Codell] brought to education make this bristling journal well worth reading."

—*Entertainment Weekly*, A-

"Remarkably unsentimental . . . The charm of this memoir is that Esmé isn't all that different from the kids . . . While you could read it as a primer on tough love, *Educating Esmé* is really a story about an unlikely bunch of kids discovering the transports of reading . . . No matter how often Hollywood gets it wrong, that's one story we never tire of."

—*Elle*

"Hilarious . . . *Educating Esmé* has won praise for its forthright depiction of an inner-city school, turning [Esmé] into one of the nation's most sought-after voices for empowering teachers—and against government-dictated curricula and testing."

—*People*

"At turns entertaining, damning, and heartbreaking, the diary is a testament to the very best and worst of teaching—to the small miracles that occur in the classroom every day, as well as the deadening bureaucracies."

—*NEA Today*

"Sassy, irrepressible and happily eccentric, Codell is the type of person who gears up for a trying day by listening to Tina Turner's 'Funkier than a Mosquita's Tweeter.'"

—*The Washington Post Book World*

"This honest and spirited account of a young teacher's experiences in a Chicago public school will warm your heart and sometimes break it."
—Chicago Tribune

"Esmé's diary of her first year and its pitfalls is funny, poignant and even sad. She gets what she wants, no matter the obstacles. Her determination to succeed, no matter the odds, is inspiring . . . An entertaining book, well worth reading."
—The Phoenix Arizona Republic

"*Educating Esmé* is a book every first-year teacher should be required to read, every in-service symposium should focus on for discussion and conflict resolution, every parent should share, and every principal should put on his or her must-read list."
—The Norfolk Virginian-Pilot

"Although it easily can be read in a single afternoon, its contents will linger in the memory long afterward. It should be read by anyone who's interested in the future of public education."
—The Boston Phoenix

"[Codell] is flighty, self-centered and appallingly self-righteous. But she is also passionate about teaching children, and you won't have to like the author to enjoy *Educating Esmé*."
—Fort Worth Star-Telegram

"What delights in this modern, true-life version of *Up the Down Staircase* is Esmé's energy . . . Her fierce enthusiasm overflows the page . . . This revealing, screamingly funny memoir offers hope and fear in equal measure to those who would teach and those who want to know about teaching."   —*Booklist*

"A spirited account . . . *Educating Esmé* is that exceptional education book about an even more exceptional teacher. It deserves to be read by anyone who cares about children."   —*Kirkus Reviews*

EDUCATING ESMÉ

EDUCATING ESMÉ

Diary
of a Teacher's
First Year

EXPANDED EDITION

Esmé Raji Codell

ALGONQUIN BOOKS
OF CHAPEL HILL
2009

All of the names of students, teachers, and administrators
herein have been changed.

Published by
ALGONQUIN BOOKS OF CHAPEL HILL
Post Office Box 2225
Chapel Hill, North Carolina 27515-2225

a division of
Workman Publishing
225 Varick Street
New York, New York 10014

Printed in the United States of America.
Published simultaneously in Canada
    by Thomas Allen & Son Limited.
Design by Anne Winslow.

Portions of this diary were originally aired on
WBEZ, Chicago, as "Call Me Madame" in the radio
Life Stories series, produced by Jay Allison.

Library of Congress Cataloging-in-Publication Data
Codell, Esmé Raji, [date]
   Educating Esmé : diary of a teacher's first year /
Esmé Raji Codell—Expanded ed.
        p. cm.
   ISBN-13: 978-1-56512-935-1
     1. Codell, Esmé Raji, [date]   2. First year teachers—
Illinois—Chicago—Diaries.   3. Elementary school
teachers—Illinois—Chicago—Diaries.   I. Title.
   LB2844.1.N4C63 2009
   372.110092—dc22
   [B]   2009016470

10 9 8 7 6 5

To Jim

FOREWORD

My grandmother liked to say, "Be sweet my child, and let who will be clever." Obviously Esmé Raji Codell never had my grandmother's dictum drummed into her young ears. As I read her diary, I found her intelligence, energy, and imagination thrilling but, unable to escape my grandmother's long reach from the grave, was from time to time alarmed by Madame Esmé's acerbic honesty. Indeed, sometimes she scared the living daylights out of me. I kept remembering my first year of teaching. At the time I fancied myself a rather daring young teacher, but what was there to fear?

The principal hardly ever made the descent from his front office to my solitary basement classroom at the rear of the school. He never caught us with the desks shoved against the walls doing broad jumps the length of the room or reading *Macbeth* instead of the language arts text. Even if he had, I think he would have been mildly amused. But let's face it, compared to Esmé, I was a staid traditionalist. I never roller-skated down the halls, never swapped places for a day with my most troublesome student. It never occurred to me to teach math by means of the cha-cha or give delightful new names to tired old subject designations. And I never asked anyone, much less the principal, to call me "Madame." No one, not even I, knew if I had had a successful day in that basement classroom, unlike Esmé, who, on February 7, rejoices over her students' depth of understanding at the culmination of their unit on Native Americans, and then proceeds to say: "Like every successful day, it seems, it ended by getting called into the office."

Esmé is an original. There is, alas, no way to clone her. More ominously, she is exactly the kind of teacher who is all too often so scary to the status quo that she is under constant threat of dismissal or, at the very least, is always having her differences questioned.

Are we then simply to read this book with delight and then close it with a sigh? After all, it was first pub-

lished to glowing reviews in 1999 when No Child Left
Behind (including its grimmer unintended consequences) wasn't yet a gleam in a bureaucrat's eye. Today
so many creative and devoted teachers not only have to
struggle against unimaginative administrations, fearful
parents, and wearied colleagues, they have also to battle
entire legislative bodies that have never taught a child
yet dare to equate educational success or failure with
the ability of fourth graders to choose one out of four
given answers to mind-numbing questions that have
nothing to do with the joy of literature or the elegance
of math. How could a penciled-in circle on an answer
sheet reveal a child's delight in the amazing stories of
people in the past? Is there anything on that sheet that
would show how this child had come to marvel at the
mysteries of the universe? Can a standardized test show
that a student has been led to wonder how everything,
including her own body, is put together? Too many
teachers have said to me that they can no longer really
teach. They must spend all their time preparing their
students for "the test." By demanding that teachers
teach "to the test" or to some narrow, proscribed curriculum, we have lost many of our brightest and best.

Esmé is unique, so what help is she to those struggling in an alien climate to be successful teachers? She gives us a clue in the argument she has with the board of education workshop leader, in which she speaks to "closed-door teacher anarchy." She is right when she says that nobody knows what is happening after the teacher closes the door. "At worst, mediocrity. At best, miracles." A prefabricated curriculum could help the mediocre teacher, she says, by giving him or her a script to follow. On the other hand, it could operate as "benign suggestions" to the truly good teacher.

So much of teaching, she reminds us, is sharing. "You can't test what sort of teacher someone will be, because testing what someone knows isn't the same as what someone is able to share. This will be different for every teacher." And then she goes on to say, "I am operating from a position where I am personally vested in my approach, which any teacher will tell you is a privileged place to be. Does being personally vested make a teacher successful? Not necessarily. Does it make a teacher accountable? Absolutely."

Madame Esmé has shared with us her idiosyncratic teaching and learning as a first-year teacher.

The often unhappy administration was impressed—
and I dare say, surprised—when the Iowa tests revealed that every student had advanced at least a year,
and some two or three years. So by the penciled-in-
circle measurement she was a successful teacher. But
no one reading this book will conclude that her students' test scores were the only, or even the most important, measure of her success. Her fifth-graders
wrote that assessment on the scarf they presented to
her on their final day. Madame Esmé cried when she
read their words, and so did I.

—Katherine Paterson

EDUCATING ESMÉ

PART I

To: fifth-grade beginniners
From: Melanie, fifth-grader

I know what your thinking your
thinking that going to the fifth grade
is going to be fun and not hard well
I got something to tell you. You
got to know every thing. you have to
know your devition your time tables
know how to do the dowy dowy decimal
sistem. There are a lot of book she
have read this year like *The Hundred
Dresses* by Eleanor Estes, *Greek Myths*,
Helen Keller, *The Bat-Poet* by Randall
Jarrell and . . . and . . . you would
find out the rest when you get here.
you can not say shut up and you must
follow the golden rule and you can not
talk in the hall and you must not talk
back at the teacher well I think that
is anouf to let you know about the 5th
grade life. Ta ta . . .

June 21

Ismene died. That's where I'll start, because it's with Ismene that my real teaching started.

I cried when I found out. I tried to go to her memorial—I mean, I went—but it was all in Greek, and everybody crossing themselves made me nervous. I couldn't really concentrate on remembering Ismene, her sharp eyes, like a sparrow. She was my guide. I would not be a teacher without her.

I'm not quite a teacher yet—that is, I haven't had a class of my own. That's in September, if I last and if the new school opens on time. I'm surprised Mr. Turner hired me, only twenty-four years old, to help him open a brand-new public school. You would think he would want someone more experienced. The interview was very brief. He asked, "How would you describe your classroom discipline style?"

I answered, "Assertive."

He said, "What does that mean?"

"It means I say what I mean and I mean what I say," I replied.

"Well, say you're having a problem with a student, how would you deal with it?"

"I would document the child's behavior and then try interventions such as using successive approximations toward our goal or home involvement, depending on the individual situation," I explained. After a silence, I added, "I wouldn't call the office every five minutes."

He closed the little notebook on his lap and announced, "You're hired."

I had to go through a perfunctory interview with a panel that asked silly questions like, "What would you do if a child were to say 'fuck' in your classroom?"

"Faint dead away!" I put my hand to my forehead.

"What kind of classroom environment will you create?"

"Do you mean the physical, emotional, or educational environment?"

"I guess I don't know."

"Then I guess I don't know how to answer you," I confessed, "but I'll offer examples of each . . ."

I was teary-eyed the whole cab ride home, thinking that I must not really want the job, to answer questions in such a cavalier manner! Why wasn't I more polite? Me and my big mouth! etc. But when I got home, there was a message from Mr. Turner: "They loved you!"

So now here I am, typing, copying, answering phones, "being flexible," as Mr. Turner calls it. I think that means doing things you're not supposed to do for longer than you ever thought you'd have to do them.

Tomorrow Mr. Turner says I should come see the graduation ceremonies at the school where he was vice-principal. They must be planning to make a hot dog out of him—I can't imagine why he'd let me stop typing for a minute, unless it was to bear witness to his glory.

. . .

July 7

I was right about the ceremony. There was another assembly, with all of the children who were coming to the new school. I approached Mr. Turner. "If you have an intention of introducing me, would you please call me Ms. Esmé rather than Mrs. Codell?"

I was surprised at how my request surprised him.

He said, "That's against board policy."

Not having been born yesterday, I replied that in all the other classrooms I had worked in, that is what the children called me.

He seemed bemused. "But it's not your legal name." He smiled helplessly.

"Certainly it is."

"Your *last* name."

"Let's pretend . . . I haven't got a last name. I'll be like . . . Sade."

He laughed heartily at this, and I laughed too, but then he said, "Well, I think we'll call you Mrs. Cordell." The way he mispronounces my last name makes me wince.

"You can call me what you like." I smiled and tried

to maintain a pleasant tone. "But we will see what name I answer to." We made eye contact. He turned away and mumbled something about "women's libbers."

He introduced me as Ms. Esmé. I felt uncomfortable. I didn't mean to be confrontational, but I think I should be able to decide what name I answer to. Mr. Turner is well-intentioned, but it is not enough. He is not clever, he is not intelligent. At least not to me.

I WROTE A proposal for a schoolwide Fairy Tale Festival. Mr. Turner approved it, but he said the idea has to first go through administrators, teachers, and community members. I showed my idea to the librarian-to-be. She was skeptical. That's typical. If you give people an idea these days, they just think you are sharing it with them so they can critique it, play devil's advocate, and so on. It doesn't occur to them that they might help or get enthused or at least have the courtesy to get out of your way. Sometimes this frustrates me, but I try deep inside to move beyond it. Sometimes I think, *Why invent projects? What is the point? How will I ever accomplish what I set out to do, what I imagine?* Then I think of the past, even before I was born, the great small feats people accomplished. I think of things like Mary Martin washing her hair onstage in *South Pacific*, or the Kungsholm puppet operas with sixty puppets onstage at once, or the palace built by the postman in France, or the circus I saw in Copenhagen where a woman wore a coat of live minks, or any of the things I enjoy and value, and I think: *Those people had to work to accomplish those things, they thought of details, they followed through.* Even if I come off as naive and zealous, even if I get on everyone's nerves, I have to follow these examples. Even if I fail, I have to try and try and try. It may be exhausting, but that is beside the point. The goal is not necessarily to succeed but to keep trying, to be the kind of person who has ideas and see them through.

We'll see. I aim too high, probably. But if I don't aim, how will I hit anywhere near the target?

July 8

I hereby attach a copy of what I expect to be a most interesting curiosity, the crowning jewel of my naiveté: my Fairy Tale Festival proposal. Perhaps I will look back on this and think, as I was most condescendingly informed yesterday at the Friends of the School Library Committee meeting (which I organized, by the way, after it was explained to me that a committee needed to be invented because a committee needs to exist to approve a proposal), that it was not realistic to do, as I would surely have known had I been teaching awhile. I said everything I proposed I was willing to coordinate, that I just needed help on the actual day of the festival to supervise for the children's safety. The vice-principal, Ms. Coil, said no, everything should be a group effort. Then, as a group, they decided they didn't want to put forth the effort. So, the end. Some of my favorite sections:

FAIRY TALE FASHION SHOW

Is fur still "in" for the Three Bears? What is Cinderella wearing to the ball this season? Miss Riding Hood still sizzles in red (ask any wolf), and Sleeping Beauty is a cutie in her pj's. The Paper Bag Princess makes a statement without saying a word, while less is more for the

Emperor's New Clothes (boxer shorts)! The possibilities are only as limited as local theaters, closet costumers, good sport volunteer models (adults and children), and our collective imaginations!

Carnival Games
Some ideas:

- Ugly Duckling Match. Find the numbers that match on the bottoms of bobbing plastic ducks in a "pond" (plastic tub).

- Three Billy Goats Gruff Toss. Three beanbags through holes in a thematically painted board wins.

Bookmarks make good inexpensive prizes. What else? Let's brainstorm!

Bake Sale/Book Sale
How about Frog Prince cupcakes (with green food-colored frosting), Thumbelina finger sandwiches, Giant's magic rings (doughnuts) or cookies from Red Riding Hood's basket? Again, volunteerism and imagination are our only limitations.

I only meant that last line to be cheerleading. I was carried away with the idea of infinite possibility. The same sense of infinite possibility, from the sour expressions on the faces of my cohorts, that would compel someone to go over Niagara Falls in a barrel. All that is really necessary, after all, is a little "volunteerism and imagination."

Another gross thing at the meeting: Lillia, a teacher from Italy, about fifty-five years old, was chatting along and came to the word "conspicuous," which she pronounced "copiscuous." Big deal!

But no. Ms. Coil made a hand gesture of a cascading waterfall beneath her chin and enunciated, "Con-SPICK-you-us."

Lillia just looked.

"Con-SPICK-you-us," the vice-principal repeated, clearly wanting Lillia to follow. Wow! Isn't that audacious! I could have smacked her across the nose!

"Yes," Lillia nodded and continued what she was saying. When she came to that word again, she said, "Co-PISS-cue-us."

Congratulate me—I didn't laugh out loud.

July 15

What's so hard about saying thank you? Mr. Turner never says it.

He tells me to come in early and tells me to stay hours late. Then he calls me up at 11:30 at night. "I have a principal's meeting tomorrow. What do I think?"

I hardly know what *I* think when it's nearly midnight, let alone what *he* thinks. Since he's my boss, I spew off some educational theory that's still fresh in my mind from college. The next day, I go to the meeting with him. When he gets up to speak, it's the exact words of a twenty-four-year-old coming out of a fifty-year-old mouth. Everyone claps. P. T. Barnum would have been proud of such a fraud.

This calling me up late at night has happened more than it should. Sometimes he calls to say, "So, I did a pretty good job today, huh!" Other times he calls to tell me how stupid he thinks the other teacher he hired is, asking, "Why can't she be more like *you*, Cordell!" (Of course mispronouncing my name.) I don't take this as a compliment at all. Who's to say he's not calling her when he's done calling me, saying how stupid *I* am?

If he were the sort of person who ever said thank you for anything, I would say, poor man, lonely man. People who don't say thank you, people who ask "What do I think?," people who call people on the phone after a twelve-hour workday, people who talk behind people's backs, well, maybe there's a reason they are lonely. But I think I cured his late-night hellos.

When the phone rang at 11:30 the night before last, I let it ring. The machine answered it, he left his name. I set my alarm clock.

At 3:00 a.m. my alarm clock rang. I called Mr. Turner.

"Oooh! Did I wake you up?"

He grunted in reply.

"I'm *so* sorry. It's just that you called me so *late*. I knew you wouldn't call me so *late* if it wasn't terribly important. So I thought I had better call you back."

Last night I had a phone-free evening.

MR. TURNER KEEPS asking this woman in her twenties to type stuff for him. Really big stuff, like school improvement plans that are as thick as the width of my thumb, and always at the last minute. She kept coming in and doing it, but finally she said, "Mr. Turner, I've got two kids at home. I had to leave a pot of macaroni and cheese on the burner. If you're going to keep calling me in to do these big projects, I'm afraid I'm going to have to ask to be compensated."

"That's all right." He snatched the pile of papers out of her hand.

"I don't mind doing it, Mr. Turner, but you've got to understand, it's very difficult for me to drop everything and . . ."

"I understand." His voice was even, too even. "It's all right. It's fine. We don't need you. You can go ahead home."

"If that's the way you feel," she said with a shrug.

After she left, Mr. Turner flew into a rage. "Compensated! Compensated! After all I've done for her!" He went on and on about owing favors and one hand washing the other and I'll wash your back you wash mine and reciprocation and how he surely would have compensated her but now that she has asked she can just forget it. He kept asking me, didn't she have the nerve and how dare she. I wanted to ask him how dare *he*, and wasn't he embarrassed to call a woman away from her family without offering to compensate her in the first place, but he was in such a fury about what she owed him for some reason that I was too nervous to speak up. So I just said, "Well, she had macaroni and cheese on the burner."

He started his tantrum at 5:30, and I didn't escape from his soliloquy until 7:30. My ears were ringing. As I lay in bed, I thought of quitting. I feel sure now that I am not working for a good person. I thought of Ismene's warning: "You are a very gifted teacher. Don't teach. Be an actress instead." I tried not to think about it.

I fell asleep remembering my last day in the class I taught with Ismene. I had made cookies for the children, brightly iced and sprinkled, in the Moravian shape of a hand with a heart in it. When the children walked down the hall to exit that day, they were all waving these cookie hands at me. Good-bye, Ms. Esmé! Good luck, Ms. Esmé!

· · ·

July 23

Ismene Siteles. Fifth-grade teacher.

I didn't think I would like her. She seemed so traditional.

"Are you married?" I asked after she asked me.

"No. I have enough children to take care of without a husband."

Gaunt and graying, she pulled ears and yelled a lot. "Absorb!" she would command. She was startling to watch, and that's what I was there to do: Watch. One hundred hours of "observation," that's the training requirement before student teaching.

On the second day, though, she squinted her penetrating eyes at me and crooked a finger, posing as if she were casting a spell. "*You*," she accused. "*You* are *ready*." That was the end of "observation." For several hundreds of hours, she let me stand in front of the children and read. Ask. Count. Laugh. Yell. Do magic tricks. Teach.

She was a harsh critic. She brought me to tears. Then she dried them. She urged me to forgive myself at the end of each day, that no single thing I could say would break a child . . . or make a child. Still, she taught me not to be too flippant, that, as a doctor cures what ails the body, I must strive to diagnose the roadblocks to learning. Thanks to her generous advice and allowances, I enter my profession with excitement instead of trepidation, and the understanding that, really, I have no right to indulge in a lack of confidence. It would only interfere with the task before me.

Ismene taught me basics: Ignoring bad behavior as long as you can stand it. Maintaining quiet lines. How a soft voice can be more effective than a loud voice. Starting out with positive comments to parents before lowering the boom. Waiting patiently for children to answer questions.

She also made me laugh.

"Where's your homework?" she asked a boy.

"Suck my dick," the boy replied.

To everything the boy replied, "Suck my dick." "Suck my dick." "Suck my dick." Every day. "Suck my dick." Ismene ignored it.

Finally, we were delivering the class to gym.

"Get in line."

"Suck my dick."

She pulled him out of line by his ear. "Come with me, Esmé. I need a witness." I followed.

She dragged him into the boy's bathroom. They faced each other. His shoulders lifted and fell in his puffy nylon jacket as he breathed forcefully, indignant about his treatment.

"Drop your pants!" She commanded.

"*What!* You can suck my dick!"

"That, sir, is *exactly* what I intend to do."

His mouth fell open with an audible plop. They stood facing each other without moving for an eternity.

At last she spoke. "All year long I've been listening to you: 'Suck my dick! Suck my dick!' Why would you ask for something so ridiculous at school? From your teacher? Either you are completely crazy or you really want me to 'suck your dick,' as you have been insisting. So drop your pants."

"No," the mortified boy quavered.

"Then in the future," she warned in a sinewy, deliberate, almost cheerful growl, "be careful what you ask for. Or a certain old lady just . . . might . . . give it to you." She leaned down and opened both her eyes as wide as they would go and grinned with all her sharp teeth.

I don't know how many weeks it was before color returned to that boy's face. I know he didn't say "Suck my dick" for the rest of the year.

She was my mentor.

I'm confident because I'm prepared.

I will kick pedagogical ass in her memory.

July 28

Mr. Turner got the idea that the businesses in the community should make contributions that could be used as incentives for the children when the new school opens. So we went together to the local business strip, Hollywood Avenue, to solicit donations. Most of the businesses there are pawnshops and smelly fried chicken huts, so I had my doubts about the success of the whole endeavor. Mr. Turner stood imposingly over six feet tall. He had donned an elegant pinstriped suit and his hair glistened. He had a prewritten sales pitch, which he enunciated mightily to each store owner as if he were reciting from Hamlet.

None of the owners of the dilapidated stores had anything they could contribute, though the owner of one of the pawnshops liked my necklace. The hairdresser at the hair weave salon locked the door when she saw Mr. Turner coming and shook her head angrily when he knocked.

I tried to make pleasant conversation. I asked him how he came to be a principal. He said the Vietnam War was going on and he felt a black man would be stupid to fight for this country, so he went to college instead. He changed his major from drama to administration so they wouldn't draft him. Then he asked if I was going to marry my boyfriend. I said I felt that was kind of personal, and that was the end of pleasant conversation.

All in all, a stupid day.

August 5

One great thing is that I get to see the school built from the ground up. The architects take us around. It's so exciting to think that soon the rooms will be filled with children! I am going to teach the fifth grade.

Today I got to see my classroom for the first time. It has a nice wide window ledge and shelves beneath so I can make displays. Only two things bugged me. One, there were four bullet holes in the window perpendicular to the chalkboard. Mr. Turner says the window will be replaced by the time the kids arrive. The other thing, which is a really weird, ungrateful thing, is that it didn't smell like a school, which is usually a kind of combination of kitchen cleanser and fish sandwiches. I love smells, and that smell in particular is one of my favorites. When I think of being a teacher, I always think of smelling that smell to my heart's content. Some fringe benefit! It just smells like sawdust and drippy pipes right now, which has its charm but is not the karma I am looking for. It makes me think, in a secret corner of myself, that I didn't pick the right school to work at. But that's just silly!

August 16

There was a meeting at the community center so everyone could meet the teachers of the new school. We were introduced one by one and then stood up behind Mr. Turner. When we were all assembled, it was apparent that there was a disproportionate amount of twenty-something slender white girls wearing short, albeit professional, skirts.

"Is this the fucking Miss America Pageant?" one of the teachers whispered to me out of the side of her mouth.

There were thirty-five of us, out of over eight hundred applicants. I helped Mr. Turner sort through the résumés. Some were handwritten and looked totally mediocre. Mr. Turner insisted we still contact everyone to be interviewed. "You can't tell if they have something to offer just from their résumés," he insisted. Tonight I figured out what it is that we all might have to offer.

September 18

Sorry I haven't written. A lot has been going on, as you can probably imagine.

Setting up my classroom, at long last, was very exciting. I put up a bulletin board with a big red schoolhouse shape *without* windows (those would come later) that said, "New School . . . You're What Makes It Special." There was a tree covered with apples. Each apple had a number on it. *Thunk, thunk, thunk,* it was so gratifying, stapling it to the board. Then I had to arrange the chairs. I noticed other teachers arranging the desks so children would be sitting in cooperative, small groups. I kept thinking that that was politically correct, I should do it like that. But somehow it took all the romance out of the first day of school, when you're supposed to feel very formal and alien, a day when your thoughts are very new and personal. So I decided to be more traditional and put the desks in rows. Besides, I want to seem really mean for a while. I bought black pointy lace-up boots, like a witch, to wear for the first day, to add to the dramatic effect.

I put up another bulletin board that said, "Solving Conflicts: 1. Tell person what you didn't like. 2. Tell person how it made you feel. 3. Tell person what you want in the future. 4. Person responds with what they can do. Congratulations! You are a Confident Conflict Conqueror!" I didn't make this up. I learned it from a Jewish guy my age I observed teaching at a Good News Christian private school. We are going to have conflict resolution meetings every Friday, to be mediated eventually by the kids. I also put up a smiley-faced mobile of "Kind Words."

The third bulletin board I made was a cutout of King Kong on top of an aluminum-foil Empire State Building, with the caption "King Kong Says Reach for the Top!" and on the floors of the Empire State it says, "Listen," "Think," Work carefully," and "Check your work." I left space to hang their best papers.

I made a "clothesline" with four articles of fake clothing made of poster board covered with ribbons and sequins and stuff, hung on a rope with clothespins. Each article of clothing has a pocket in back that holds either a fun puzzle or artwork activity or an at-your-desk game. Across the clothes is written "If . . . you . . . finish . . . early."

There is a spelling center with spelling games, a typewriter, an electric wiggle pen, a box of cornmeal and sponge letters with tempera paint for kids to practice their spelling words. There is also an art center with bins of new, juicy markers, craft books and real art books with pictures of naked people (isn't it nice to have books where the penises and breasts are already drawn in!), and goodies such as glitter, old wrapping paper, colored glues.

My *pièce de résistance* is my 3D papier mâché poster with five multiethnic kids' heads sticking out that says, "Welcome to Cool School." One of the kids is wearing a real pair of purple sunglasses. I like the girl with steel-wool red hair. I had to make the kids' heads out of wire first. It took a lot of work to make, but it is gorgeous, if I do say so myself. If I was a kid and saw this, I would just die.

The older teachers shook their heads and told me my room looked overstimulating, which means they are totally jealous because I have the most insanely beautiful classroom ever, of all time. Oh, God! I have beautiful portraits of explorers over the chalkboard, the cloakroom has a cutout panorama of an international open-air market, and there's a learning center with flags of all nations. I'm sorry, this room is so fun it's sickening. I feel sorry for any kid who is not in this room.

So, FIRST DAY. As they entered, they each took a numbered apple off of the bulletin board and matched it to the numbered apples taped to the desks. This is how they were seated temporarily. I passed out my list of necessary supplies, in English and Spanish. Of the thirty kids, all were black except for about five Mexican kids and one girl who is from Pakistan and one from the Philippines. Then I looked them over and thought, *This is my destiny, to have this group of children before me. As they were growing, aging to be fifth graders, I was training, and now we meet, in this unique place and time.* The moment felt holy.

I gave them my speech about how mean I was and how I've taught football players and cowboys and dinosaurs and Martians, so a few fifth graders aren't *too* challenging, but I need the money, so I'd give it a shot. I told them that they were going to work harder than they ever have in their whole lives, so if they want extra credit, they should get a head start on sweating. I told them if they didn't have their supplies by Monday, they already will have earned a check on their report card for preparedness. I showed them my one Golden Rule: "Treat others the way you would like to be treated," written out in gold glitter.

Then I gave them red and white paper and showed

them how to make a little book that looks like a window. Inside they each wrote and illustrated a little composition, "Old School, New School," about how they liked where they came from and how they felt coming here. Then I hung their work on the big red schoolhouse cutout on the bulletin board, so now the school had little windows you could open and read.

Here are two of my favorites:

"I was so scare I hide under the bed [drawing of two eyes under the bed]. And then I meet nice teacher [drawing of me with curly hair and pearls, smiling ear to ear—after all the trouble I went to to be nasty!]."

"My name is Samantha. And I like my old school because I liked old teachers from 0-4. When I first started school she was mean. But then when I got to know she was nice. And all the other teacher I thought was mean. But once got to know them they were nice. And now I's the New School with a new teacher. And she says she's the meanest teacher in the west but I know she's not. I think just saying that to make us good, kind."

. . .

September 20

I took a cassette-recorded sample of each of the children's oral reading abilities. Some of them don't have a real grasp of phonetics. They can't really comprehend what they're reading because they are preoccupied with guessing the sound each letter is supposed to make. It was sometimes painful to see these big kids struggling, reading from books they chose, books they felt good about. So I told them we are making an alphabet museum . . . for the kindergartners. Each day the kids are assigned a letter, and the following day they bring in interesting things they find beginning with that letter. Then we go through each letter as the children present their items. We go through the sounds, "rehearsing" for the little kids. We are learning an alphabet song by Carole King, "Alligators All Around," which they are going to present. We are going to make displays for each letter on twenty-six desks, using the stuff the kids bring in. A kid will be behind each desk, and two kids will greet the children at the door, and two kids will be reading ABC books to visitors who finish viewing the displays, so everyone will have a job. The best part is, my fifth graders are getting their needed alphabet practice without having to feel ashamed. After all, it's not their fault.

Vanessa, who can barely read or write, really likes learning the sign-language alphabet. She is very proud that she can spell her name with it. I told her she could teach the deaf someday.

September 26

I set up a classroom library. We don't use the reading textbook. What for? Grown-ups don't read textbooks unless they're forced. I told them we could read real books so long as they don't steal any. I make a big show of counting the books at the end of the day. The kids sigh audibly when they're all there. They look beautiful, like a bookstore, facing out in a big wooden display my uncle made for me. Plus, it covers the bullet-riddled window that never was repaired.

We don't call the subjects the old-fashioned names in Room 211. Math is "Puzzling," science is "Mad Scientist Time," social studies is "T.T.W.E.," which stands for "Time Travel and World Exploring," language arts is "Art of Language," and reading is "Free Reading Time." I did this because I figured kids at this age come to me with preconceived notions of what they are good at. This way, a kid who thinks she's no good in math might turn out to be good at Puzzling, and so on.

In the morning, three things happen religiously. I say good morning, real chipper, to every single child and make sure they say good morning back. Then I collect "troubles" in a "Trouble Basket," a big green basket into which the children pantomime unburdening their home worries so they can concentrate on school. Sometimes a kid has no troubles. Sometimes a kid piles it in, and I in turn pantomime bearing the burden. This way, too, I can see what disposition the child is in when he or she enters. Finally, before they can come in, they must give me a word, which I print on a piece of tagboard and they keep in an envelope. It can be any word, but preferably one that they heard and don't really know or one that is personally meaningful. A lot of times the kids ask for *Mississippi*, just to make me spell it. We go over the words when we do our private reading conferences. I learned this from reading *Teacher* by Sylvia Ashton-Warner, who taught underprivileged Maori children in New Zealand. She says language should be an organic experience. I love her approach.

It takes a long time to get in the door this way, but by the time we are in, I know every kid has had and given a kind greeting, has had an opportunity to learn something, and has tried to leave his or her worries on the doorstep. Some kids from other classrooms sneak into our line to use the Trouble Basket or to get a word card.

Then the national anthem blares over the intercom. The kids sing with more gusto now that we shout "Play ball!" at the end. We do Puzzling until 10:30, then we alternate Mad Sciencing with T.T.W.E., lunch, reading aloud, Free Reading and journaling, and Art of Language.

At the end of the day, as the kids exit, they fill in the blanks as I call out, "See you in the _____ [morning!]." "Watch out for the _____ [cars!]." "Don't say _____ [shut up!]." "I love _____ [you!]." This is a game I played with my father at bedtime growing up. It gives the day a nice closure.

WE HAD OUR first conflict resolution meeting. I explained that I would mediate only the first two meetings, then it was their time, and that I would not interfere unless there was an emergency. I explained some ground rules: Only the mediators and people involved in the conflict could speak. The rest were there for support. We do not argue about what happened in the past but discuss what we desire for the future. We will follow the steps on the bulletin board. After conflicts are resolved, we will go around and give affirmations, that is, say something nice we noticed about each other. Ozzie raised his hand to have a conflict resolved with Ashworth.

"What happened that you didn't like?"

"He . . ."

"No, we're not telling on people. Tell him, 'I didn't like it when you . . .'"

Ozzie nodded. "Ashworth, I didn't like it when you tried to kiss me."

Laughter. I tried to model composure. The class collected itself.

"And how did this make you feel?"

"It made me feel gay."

Off to a running start.

September 27

After lunch each day I read aloud to them. We push the desks out of the way, pull down the shades, and turn off all the lights, except for an antique Victorian desk lamp I have. It is a very cozy time.

I was reading them *The Hundred Dresses* by Eleanor Estes, about a Polish immigrant girl who is so poor that she wears the same dress to school every day but insists that she has a hundred dresses lined up in her closet. The girls tease her mercilessly until she moves away. Her antagonists discover that she really did have a hundred dresses . . . a hundred beautiful *drawings* of dresses. Oh, God, it took everything not to cry when I closed the book! I especially like that the story is told from the teaser's point of view.

Well, everything was quiet at the end, but then Ashworth asked if he could whisper something in my ear. He whispered, "I have to tell the class something," and discreetly showed me that he was missing half of a finger. It was a very macabre moment, but I didn't flinch.

I faced him toward the class and put my hands on his shoulders. He was trembling terribly. "Ashworth has something personal to share with you. I hope you will keep in mind *The Hundred Dresses* when he tells you."

"I . . . I only have nine and a half fingers," he choked. "Please don't tease me about it." He held up his hands.

The class hummed, impressed, then was silent as Ashworth shifted on his feet. Finally, Billy called out, "I'll kick the ass of anyone who makes fun of you!"

"Yeah, me too!" said Kirk.

"Yeah, Ash! You just tell us if anyone from another class messes with you, we'll beat their ass up and down!"

Yeah, yeah, yeah! The class became united in the spirit of ass-kicking. Ashworth sighed and smiled at me. The power of literature!

. . .

September 29

New girl, Esther, from Haiti. Dark, eyes darting, frightened. "She's got a record of fighting from her other school," Ms. Coil explained. Who asked her?

"*Salut, mon amie!*" I welcomed her. Her shoulders dropped, relaxed. Her smile is beautiful and full of mischief.

THE KIDS LIKE something new I made: the Thinking Cap. It's an oversized hat made of prismatic gold paper, with a long prismatic paper tree coming out about two feet off of the top. It says THINKING CAP in black press-on letters across the front. Kids who need more time to give a good answer use it. The kids have become very thoughtful since it's been introduced.

September 30

Shira is Filipino and speaks mostly Tagalog. Sometimes she goes into fetal position under her desk. She has four brothers, named Vincent I, Vincent II, Vincent III, and Vincent IV.

Today Shira was crying because she felt Twanette took her pen. Twanette said no, it was her pen, she got it for 10¢ at Walgreen's. The pen looked more expensive than that, so I didn't really believe it. Plus, I know those kind are sold in sets. And finally, Shira had work in her notebook in that pink ink.

After school, Shira's stepfather came in and told me that Shira complained that Twanette took Shira's menstrual pad out of the garbage in the bathroom and showed it to other girls.

Twanette also chews big wads of gum and took neon green glue she was not supposed to use and gooped up a whole table, almost ruining some expensive books.

So when I saw Twanette's mom had come to pick her up after school, I asked to talk with her. I started by telling her that Twanette has really been improving in completing her work and that I was proud of her efforts. Then I told her the rest, explaining that I hadn't actually seen the menstrual pad thing but that the father complained and we had to be extra sensitive because Shira had been in the country only a couple of months and had trouble speaking up for herself.

Right about then, the mom started wonking Twanette over the head with a rolled-up magazine she was holding. She assured me that she would whip Twanette with a belt at home, adding apologetically that she usually whips Twanette every six months, but she's been behind schedule.

When I suggested that perhaps a belt would not be effective in changing Twanette's attitude, the mom assured me, "Twanette's attitude's gone change after this, believe you me, you won't have *no* more problems with *this* girl!"

Twanette was hysterical and denying everything. Mom called her a "big dork" and other things. It was very depressing, and I felt responsible. I acted very calm, but when they left I dry-heaved into the wastebasket. I felt like hell.

I hope Twanette doesn't shoot me tomorrow for telling on her.

October 1

Twanette didn't shoot me today. She wrote me a thank you note for saying something good about her to her mom. We also had the alphabet museum. Three kindergarten classes came through. It was a big success.

The kids keep journals. They can write in them during Free Reading if they choose. If they don't want me to read something, they put an E with a circle and a line through it at the top of the page, a symbol for "No Esmés allowed." I read them anyway, but I don't tell. I find out interesting things. For instance, Ashworth was upset all day because I wore pants, and I never wear pants. He thought his real teacher must have been abducted by aliens.

October 5, my birthday

Terrible thing. Somebody stole the Columbus comic book. I said, "Whoever did it, just put it back," but nobody did. So after school I took the whole library down and shoved it in the closet and locked it. The kids noticed right away the next morning.

"I told you if you stole from me, I'd take it all back. I'm not a liar."

"That's not fair," one girl complained. "We didn't *all* steal the book!"

"No, I'll tell you what's not fair. My working Saturdays so that you can read real literature and then having the books stolen from under my nose. That's *really* not fair. I only share with *friends*. I'm not going to leave my personal possessions out when I can't trust the people I'm with. Would you?"

Nobody answered. I passed out the reading textbooks. The children complained noisily. "You're getting what the rest of the school gets," I reminded them. "I don't see what's the problem."

The mood was grim for the rest of the day. I thought, *They have good taste. They know this is boring.*

But I'm worried. What if I never get the book back? Am I going to have to teach reading like this all year? I have to be consistent with my threat, or they will never believe me again. I'll have no discipline. I won't be able to teach anything.

GOD, KID! GIVE ME BACK THE STUPID BOOK AND LET ME TEACH YOU THE BEST WAY I KNOW HOW!

I'm so disappointed. It was a struggle not to cry in front of them.

October 7

Still no Columbus comic. I wore an ugly blue poly-ester suit, very cold and businesslike. We worked from textbooks all day. If they want a typical classroom experience, they're going to get one!

After school, Valerie's mom came to see me in the office. "Valerie's been depressed since you took the books down," she said. "I'm going to insist you put them back up."

"I'm sorry she's depressed," I said. "Frankly, I'm pretty depressed myself. But you are not in a position to insist I put the books back. The books belong to me, not the school, and I'm not going to put them up until I feel the children can be trusted."

"Are you saying you don't trust the children?" Her eyebrows raised.

Her eyebrows really raised when I answered, "Absolutely not! They are ten years old! They are still learning right from wrong."

"Why haven't you taught them right from wrong?" she asked angrily.

"I've imparted as much morality as I feel I have the

authority to impart, but seeing as it's only been a month, I doubt if anyone's ready to receive the Nobel Peace Prize."

"I take them to church. My baby doesn't steal."

"I'm sure that's wonderful," I said. "I certainly don't mean to imply that Valerie took the comic book, Mrs. Jackson. Please don't take this personally. I'm delighted that Valerie has enjoyed the library, and nobody would be happier than I to return it. But it is my prerogative. If you would like to work every Saturday to create a library that may or may not disappear, piece by piece, I welcome you to do so. I choose not to. Until I am given a reason to change my mind, Valerie will get what the school has entitled her to, what all the other fifth graders get, and if you wish to supplement it, go to the public library." I felt cold, but I was truly very angry. She insists that I put the books back! God, these parents don't have a clue!

Surprisingly, Valerie's mom softened. "As long as you don't think *she* took it."

"I can tell you really care about your daughter," I remarked. "If everybody cared about their kids this way, maybe we wouldn't be having this conversation." I was placating her, but I didn't want to fight anymore. Go away, feel better, and leave me to this problem.

October 8

I walked into the classroom. The comic book was sitting in the middle of my desk.

Returned.

THANK YOU, GOD!!!

October 9

Good news! Connie Porter, author of the "Addy" books in the American Girls children's historical fiction series, is coming to our school on her national tour. Ours is the only Chicago public school she will visit! I arranged it through the children's bookstore where I used to work, since she was going to do a book-signing there. The publisher was very agreeable, especially since our school is almost all black and Addy is a black character, "determined to be free in the midst of the Civil War" (that's what it says on the back of the book). They are going to send us an Addy doll worth nearly a hundred dollars to give away and are sending several Addy books so teachers can prepare their classes for the visit. Mr. Turner says we can have an assembly just so long as I take care of everything and he doesn't have to think about it.

I'm excited! I am going to start an American Girls club after school. Maybe other teachers will want to start them with their classes, too.

October 13

I planned to take some students over to a university science fair for children, where we would display our burglar alarm for school backpacks. The field trip was in the evening. I took Kyle and Samantha home with me between school and the trip, because their parents couldn't accompany them but they wanted to go. We baked a cake and had a nice little tea party. "Not too much sugar, please," Kyle wagged a finger. "Gotta watch my figure."

At the school that evening, we got on a school bus to ride to the fair. The bus was converged upon by gang members, who were throwing rocks at the windows. I watched the windows tremble, the loud cracking, right next to the children's heads (some of them were only four years old, accompanying older siblings). It was terrifying, there were so many around the bus. They looked old, even my age. Whether they would start shooting at us crossed my mind. It seemed illogical, but I felt afraid. I recognized one eighth-grade boy from our school in the rabble as he threw a rock. I felt angry. The bus pulled away. I felt very, very angry.

Mr. Turner was there, watching the whole thing from his office window, but he didn't do anything.

So the next day, with teacher permission, I confronted Perry, the one boy I recognized. "I know nothing's going to happen to you for what you did last night," I said, "but I want you to know that I saw what you did, and I didn't like what I saw."

"What?"

"You tell me what."

"You mean the bus? I didn't . . . it was . . ." Denial.

I spoke softly. "Perry, it was you. Your rocks smashed next to the heads of small children. You did an evil thing."

"It wasn't me! It was . . ."

"When you've got the guts to face what you did and talk about it, I've got the time to talk to you. But I don't have time to waste talking to a cowardly little boy." I didn't say it mean, just matter-of-factly.

He turned back to his classroom, picked up a desk, and threw it. He looked at me, his chest heaving, his eyes wet. I just shook my head, shrugged, and walked away.

The school counselor said later that Perry was crying half the day, begging to be let out of class to see me. He told her he had to apologize for something. I wonder?

October 15

Showed *The Miracle Worker*. The kids liked the part where Annie Sullivan and Helen are duking it out over the dinner table. I was jealous that Annie gets to smack her students and I have to be nice. I cried at the end. The kids thought that was funny. I am going to show classic movies after school every two weeks. I am building a marquee with my uncle. I got in trouble for having popcorn in class.

October 19

HOW TO FOLD A PAPER SNOWFLAKE
(For Brandi)

I can't seem to smile at Ricky
After what he said about my Mama being white
(Even if it was true)
And when Willie peed on the coats,
I just didn't want to eat lunch with him anymore
(Am I supposed to force myself?)
Vanessa's been telling me she'll kick my ass
For a week now
(Why doesn't she just *do* it?)
and now, Terry brought the gun,
Just for show, but still,
It gives me a shivery feeling to know it's there,
In his backpack, snoring,
Coughing small gray clouds of death as it dreams,
Dreams of me, perhaps.
"Are there any questions?"

My teacher is pleasant enough, smiling generously,
The cherubs of all the good advice she's embraced

46

Still tickling her beneath her armpits.
Is that all it would take:
To just say no, to just get along,
And I could be like her? Know everything
About the Colonies,
The way plants grow,
How to fold a paper snowflake?

October 21

Asha's mama came in to complain that I told the kids
they should all have their own dictionaries. She said
they are too expensive. I know Asha's dad is under in-
house arrest for burglary from what Asha writes in
her journal, but I didn't let on that I knew. I just said,
"Couldn't Asha's father pick one up on his way home
from work sometime?" I looked at her real hard, and
she looked at me real hard.

Today Asha has a real nice hardcover *Webster's New
World* dictionary. You can tell she feels good having it.
Thank you to the donor.

. . .

October 25

Esther hasn't fist-fought anyone since she's been in my room, but she keeps putting voodoo spells on people. It was funny at first, but now it's making the kids a little spooked. I called in her father for a conference. He mostly speaks French, so he brought Esther's religious tutor to translate. The tutor wore a long brightly colored mu-mu and an elaborate headdress. He looked very striking, like a king.

I told him that I was pleased with the progress Esther was making academically, but socially she had to stop putting voodoo spells on people.

The tutor laughed disarmingly. "Oh, don't worry! She can't work the magic yet!"

I explained that regardless of whether the spells were actually taking effect, I felt it was inappropriate for her to be having religious practices in our secular setting. "This way, everyone is equal. Christians, Jews . . ."

"Jews! Ha-ha! *Jews!*" This was very funny, for some reason. They were still laughing as they left, and both shook my hand warmly. The tutor promised that Esther would not cast any more spells in class.

Esther really is doing very well. During Free Reading Time she pores over *Betsy~Tacy* and *Mysterious Marie Laveau, Voodoo Queen of the Mississippi,* a book I picked up in New Orleans. Esther is my secret favorite.

October 29

Ms. Tyler was the only other teacher interested in starting an after-school club. She's doing it with her third graders. I'm doing it with my fifth graders, and some fourth- and sixth-grade teachers are reading the Addy book aloud to their classes. My club is making necklaces like the one mentioned in the book. The publisher sent boxes of fun promotional junk, like buttons, balloons, magazines, paper dolls, and bookmarks. We are going to make an Addy goody bag for all of the four hundred-some kids who will attend the assembly. We are putting Addy posters all over the school. I am getting a teeny bit sick of Addy already.

Ms. Federman is being so helpful, cutting out paper doll decorations for the Commons Area. I said I wished we had a red carpet to roll out for the author, and Ms.

Tyler got a remnant from her friend in the carpet business! It's nice to have helping hands.

MRS. RAE SAID that she was talking about slavery in her fourth-grade classroom. She told us that when she said the Jews were once slaves in Egypt, a kid asked, "Are Jews white?"

"Some Jewish people are."

"White people were slaves!" the boy cried, and the children rose to their feet in a standing ovation that, according to her, she could not subdue for five solid minutes. She said it gave her the total shivers.

November 1

Halloween was fun, though it snuck up quickly. During the past two weeks we read *The Bat-Poet* by Randall Jarrell and studied bats. We also read *The Devil and Mother Crump* and stories from *Raw Head, Bloody Bones: African American Tales of the Supernatural*. There are so many good ghosty stories, and the kids never seem to get their fill.

We graphed favorite candy and other Halloweeny

stuff in math, worked on our leaf identification scrap-books, had a scary story contest (the kids wrote such gory ones, it was a little unnerving), a pumpkin deco-rating contest, a mummy wrapping race, estimated candy corn in a jar, performed our dramatization of the book *Old Devil Wind* for the kindergarten class, and I dressed up as a witch and fielded questions about the history of Halloween. I passed out what looked like candy at the end of the day, but really it was rubber lizards and cockroaches wrapped in col-ored foil. The teacher gets in a trick!

November 2

We are studying inventors. While the kids were at gym I dressed up in an outfit with all sorts of weird stuff sticking out: rubber bands, gum, chocolate chip cook-ies, lightbulbs, with a tag attached to each item saying who invented it. I wore roller skates, too. The kids loved it when I came rolling down the hall to pick them up! Then we all made a bulletin board of lightbulb cutouts, with illustrations of famous discoveries in the middle of each bulb. The board has the heading "Bright Ideas."

Mr. Turner was nervous when he saw me. But I'm good at roller-skating. Boy, he would have been really nervous during my science magic show, if he had seen me put a piece of paper I had set on fire in a bottle to illustrate Bernoulli's Principle! Of course, I had a fire extinguisher near. But certain people just think it's their job to freak out. As long as they're freaking out, they feel busy, like they must be doing work. Getting upset is force, but no motion. Unless we are moving the children forward, we aren't doing work.

Mr. Turner gets mad when I say, "I don't work for you, I work for the children." But it's true. Isn't it?

I'll find out when I get fired, I guess.

November 3

Assembly today. National anthem. *Oh, no,* I thought. *Will they . . .?*

". . . land of the free and the home of the brave!" A small group of voices enthusiastically added the post-script. "Play ball!"

Mr. Turner stepped up to the mike. "All right, who did that!" Nobody peeped.

They had no homework today, as reward for showing good judgment when it counted most.

November 5

The Connie Porter event was a rip-roaring success. Both my and Ms. Tyler's clubs met Ms. Porter outside the school with the sign and the red carpet and flowers. All the children wore *kente* cloth headbands and ties we had made to honor Addy's African roots. Then both clubs had lunch with the author, rotating seats so that all members had some time beside her. The lunch lady was very accommodating, giving all members teacher's lunches—*oohh-la-la!*—with a Southern-style chicken menu I had arranged with her.

The classrooms then came for the assembly. There was a big display of the Addy doll and all her accessories and the Addy books and displays of children's artwork featuring the scenes from the book that children thought were most exciting. I gave the classrooms poster board and yardsticks, so they made signs, WE LOVE CONNIE PORTER! It was a real rally. As kids entered, they put their names in one box for the

Addy doll raffle if they wanted, and there was another box for the children's questions, which she would draw at random to answer.

I was worried how the classes would behave during the assembly. At one assembly, an actress playing Shirley Chisolm became so disgusted with their manners that she took off her glasses and started screaming at them. But you could hear a pin drop as Ms. Porter read from her book and then answered questions. It was wonderful that most of the children were familiar with and liked her writing. You could tell that they considered her an important guest.

It was absolutely perfect until Mr. Turner got up and started blithering his nickel's worth. He is very long-winded. Then Ms. Porter drew the name for the doll. It was a boy's name, a boy who was in Ms. Tyler's after-school club. The boy ran up onstage. Mr. Turner took the mike and the doll from Ms. Porter. He hemmed and hawed. "Well, this is highly unusual! A boy!"

It dawned on me, what that homophobic, backward idiot was going to do. He wanted to redraw a name until he got a girl! After all these weeks of work, he was going to put a damper on this event! *Don't even,* a voice screamed inside my head! I jumped onto the stage, and without even thinking, took the mike. I'll give him "highly unusual"!

"Yes, a boy, a boy who has been coming to Ms. Tyler's Addy after-school club regularly! What luck that someone so deserving, such a big Addy and Connie Porter fan should receive this prize!" I took the doll from Mr. Turner and gave it to the beaming young man. Who cares? Mr. Turner didn't put this event together, I did. So why should he get to give the doll away?

The hall was filled with begrudging applause from those who didn't win as the boy was hugged by the author, and then enthusiastic applause when they heard they were all going to get Addy treats, and then thundering applause to thank Connie Porter.

There was a book-signing after the assembly for kids who brought money to purchase books. It was worth the effort when I saw kids lined up a city block for an author's autograph. The publisher donated a hundred signed books for the poorer children, which I gave to the school counselor to distribute. The publicist said this was one of the nicest school events she's seen. Ms. Porter signed a book for me: "Thank you! Thank you! You did such a wonderful job of motivating the children. You made me feel so welcome. The world should be filled with teachers with your energy and imagination!"

Wasn't that nice?

What also would be nice would be a thank you from Mr. Turner for all those unpaid after-school hours I spent promoting the book and the event. Not that I need it, I would have done it anyway . . . I *did* it anyway. It just seems like common courtesy. Instead, he seems to be brooding. Oh, well, you can't have everything . . . just everything that counts.

November 10

"I have asked you to refrain from having the children at the school address you as Madame Esmé. If you would like for the children to refer to you by your first name with the more acceptable title of Ms., Mrs., or Miss I have no objection. I hope that in the near future you will honor my request." I look at the memo.

The children call me Madame Esmé. There is no good reason for that title. It was just a present I gave myself that first day of school, a little reward for having taken everything so seriously for so long, to have gotten from one side of the teacher's desk to the other. It is a bone of contention with my principal. In a closed-door conference in his office, Mr. Turner has told me that the name distracts from the learning process. I told him if the children can't handle the idea that people have different names, why don't we just throw in the towel right now?

In fact, the children can handle it. Once, in the middle of Puzzling, Selena called out, "Why you called *'Madame'?* Why aren't you called *Mrs.*, like everybody else?"

"Because I'm not everybody else," I explained. I wrote some titles on the board.

"*Mrs.* is short for mistress, and I'm nobody's mistress. I'm too old for *Miss,* and if I said *Ms.,* most of you would call me Mrs. by accident, and that would get on my nerves. I have to hear my name called about a thousand times a day, so it better be one that I like. So please call me Madame, *Mme.,* which is French for *my lady*. Madame Esmé, at your service. Every time I hear my name, I feel regal, like a queen. I lift up my chin and put my shoulders back, and close my eyes halfway, like I'm half-amused and half-suspicious." I demonstrated.

"You look like a giraffe," Billy remarked.

"Well, when I grow up, I'm going to be a Mrs., like my mama," said Latoya, sticking out her chin.

"That's fine," I said. "Madame was my personal preference. When you grow up, you can decide exactly what you'd like to be called.

"In *Island of the Blue Dolphins,* Karana has two names. She doesn't tell her secret name to white people, because she knows her true name is powerful and can be used against her. I tell you my true title, and my power is in that name. When you call me Madame with respect, it makes me strong enough to try to become all I want to be. When you use it with disrespect, I am weakened."

"I'm going to be a Ms.," decided Zowela, "and you people just *better* pronounce it *right*."

"I'm going to be a Mrs.," announced Melissa.

"I'm going to be a Mrs., too," squeaked Kirk. The class laughed.

"I think," said Selena slowly, "that I will be a Madame."

The class said nothing more. They returned to work.

I WAS NOT always the grand Madame I am today. I grew up in Uptown Chicago, the "inner city."

I remember being a little girl in a rented apartment, one in a six-flat, with my little brother and divorced father. It was owned by a landlord who would sit and catch flies on the back porch, then remove their wings. He admitted that it was his great dream to someday start a wingless fly circus. He died before this ambition could be realized. He left his widow, a frightful Greek Harpy named Leda, to run building operations after his passing. She had oily black hair that hung like a jagged fence around her shoulders and a face as feminine as a heavyweight boxer's. I assumed he had purchased her from a catalog.

When she wasn't axing an apple tree with children

still screaming in the boughs or throwing kittens out of third-story windows like water balloons, she was paying my father a visit to offer her insight into home decorating. Her main complaint was the books. Everywhere. In every room. Kafka! Sartre! Seuss! Kant! Kierkegaard! Aggghhh! The sight of them sent her raving, screaming that if we did not get rid of them, she would take our refrigerator away! My brother and I stood by politely and looked at each other from the corners of our eyes. Our refrigerator had not worked in months. We waited a moment for her to remember this.

"Well, then . . . I will charge you, Meester!" She leered at my father. "I will charge rent for every book that you have living here!"

It does not make sense to say something does not make sense to someone who does not make sense, but sometimes, what else can you say?

"That doesn't make any sense!" my father shouted.

"What you running here, anyway, Meester? A whorehouse?"

"A what?"

"Look at all these books, Meester! It looks like a

whorehouse! A WHORE! HOUSE! If you running whorehouse, I charge extra!"

"Don't you mean a library?" I offered, my brother making laughing noises through his nose.

"YOU *chut opp!* If I say whorehouse, I mean whorehouse!"

"Get out," my father growled, his fists balled. Years later, he would laugh at Leda, but not then. Nothing spoils a sense of humor like a divorce and a bitchy landlady.

Leda stormed past me as I held open the door. "If you live in a whorehouse, you'll grow up to a be a whore," she warned in a whisper.

"A library," I corrected, patiently.

"Okay, then! If you live in a library, you'll grow up to be a whore!"

I knew about whores, anyway. They were the ones I heard screaming all through the neighborhood in the middle of the night, when plainclothes policemen had sex with them and then put them under arrest. Once in a while I saw them in the day, wearing lamé and lace and high, high heels. I thought it was wonderful, the way they always looked like they were going to a party.

The way they sassed the patrons they didn't like. The way they seemed to know so much. A little like librarians.

Hence, my lack of offense when, during student teaching, Zahid told me I dress like a whore. I had to consider, he's from the city, too. Maybe he means it as a compliment. I answered, "Thank you."

Hence, my patience in the face of Mr. Turner's assault on "Madame."

"I know you think it's the name of someone who runs a whorehouse," I say cheerfully, "but there are other meanings. Madame Montessori, for instance, was not a whore, as far as I know."

"Well, I have the children's best interests at heart."

"Really? From where I sit, I don't think it has to do with the children at all. This is just a power trip. This whole thing is stupid, it's not about 'madame' at all, it's about you telling me to do something for no reason and me doing it. You just want to see me pucker up."

"I'll have you *written* up," he barks, stands up, sits down, stands up, points upward to the imaginary heavenly bureaucrat to whom he plans to send his complaint. "It will go on your permanent record."

"Is that the same record upon which my seventh grade misbehavior in gym is documented?" I feign concern.

"I've received legal consultation. If you refer to yourself as 'madame' again, I'm warning you, I'll pursue a court case."

"Really? Well, when I called the ACLU, they seemed to think that you're the silly one."

"The ACLU?" His eyebrows draw up fearfully. "Is that the teacher's union? You didn't call the teacher's union, did you?"

November 17

JoEllen's mom says there's a lot less fighting at their house since JoEllen taught them conflict resolution. That was nice to hear!

Letter from Selena to her dad and stepmother:

"In our class I learned so much about social studies like, slavery, Pilgrims, and how in the 1600's people lived. I understand how you two said that my teacher is really nice but sometimes she's not but there's always a reason. And I learned much more when she was screaming!"

November 19

The kids like the Greek myths. We've been studying them for a few weeks. They were impressed that Cronus ate his children. I think some of them have fathers who have dispositions like Cronus. They loved the story of the kidnapping of Persephone, especially when I ripped open the pomegranate, fruit of the dead, and red juice dribbled down my wrists. Ohhhhhh!

They are tracing and cutting out the shape of their bodies and coloring them in — creating themselves as their favorite gods. This dispelled some of their anger that none of the Greek gods were black. In the middle, they are attaching compositions of who is the god they can most relate to and why. I am waiting for a parent to accuse me of having them worship false idols. Mr. Turner walked in as all thirty-one kids were on the floor, laughing, cutting, and coloring in a fabulous mess. They didn't stop because he entered.

"There's no control!" he mourned.

"There absolutely is!" I raised my thumb, which is the signal for attention, and like a magic trick, within twelve seconds every mouth was closed, thirty-one thumbs were in the air to show they got my signal, and all eyes were on us.

"Just checking," I explained. The kids went back to work.

It's not that I'm so great or that they love me so much. It's just that I'm consistent, and they know if they do not follow my guidelines, I will be a dragon lady. Still, I loved seeing Mr. Turner's face just then.

November 22

Solved the keeping-track-of-my-classroom-library conundrum, since it is a pain to count the books each day, and the kids become stressed when there's a miscount. Now, to look at one of my books during free reading, the kid must offer up some collateral; preferably a shoe. I figure they won't leave without their shoe, which they get back when they return the book. The kids thought this was very funny and fair.

This will work great, I think. At least until we have a fire drill.

December 8

Santa Claus is coming to town, but you wouldn't know it here. The kids have been maniacs, and I find myself running more of a charm school than a fifth-grade classroom, in a Sisyphus-like effort to keep them from the bloodshed, slander, and creative abuse that so titillates them. I don't know how such poor, underprivileged children can be such spoiled brats, but there it is.

I broke up a huge fight between two eighth-grade girls I didn't know. It was the kind where kids are rolling and fingers are so entangled in one another's hair that it verges on intercourse. Well, everyone was standing around, grown-ups included. I jumped over the hedge and by the grace of God somehow broke it up. I was holding two furious children, nearly my height, by the scruffs of their puppy necks. They were still growling at each other. "Get Mr. Turner," I implored, but nobody moved a muscle to help me or get help. When I saw that, I just put the kids in their lines and gave warnings in a low, psychotic, burning-fuse tone that I am perfecting. Additionally, I squinted my eyes with one of them kind of twitching. It's quite intimidating, I'm proud to say. The girl started giving me an attitude, but I crazy-squinted her into submission like a real Svengali. When I was walking my line of kids in, a lady said, "Wow, that was some fight you broke up!"

"I could have used some help!" I barked. What the hell are grown-ups for, anyway?

December 13

Shira heard "I Saw Mommy Kissing Santa Claus" as I was trying to find something on a cassette. She came out of a fetal position and started to dance in front of the whole class, shaking and everything, with all these Polynesian-like hand movements. All of us watched in utter astonishment. When she finished, we went wild with applause. She did it again and again and again, crying and laughing at the same time. It was the weirdest thing. Then she hugged me. It was like she had a rebirth experience via "I Saw Mommy Kissing Santa Claus." She has not gone into a fetal position since and does not cry as much and is making all sorts of friends, smiling all the time.

"It's like Helen Keller's '*wa-wa*,'" JoEllen observed.

It is the weirdest thing.

December 14

Some kids broke into our room while we were out at the Christmas assembly practice. The front of the room was in disarray, but the only thing they stole was my Happy Box, the pretty box I decorated when I was a teenager and decided I wanted to be a teacher. I kept stickers and erasers and Gummi Bears and junk in it to reward kids who had a clever moment. Now it's gone. I felt sad and sentimental but said I was just glad to know it wasn't one of my students.

Ruben wrote me a letter.

"I hope you feel better about the Happy Box. I feel real good about you not losing your temper. You are the best teacher I have ever had."

God! His writing is improving!

I offered a reward over the intercom for the return of my box. Till then, some girls made me a new one from a pencil box. That was nice.

December 17

We had our Christmas assembly. It was supposed to be an international theme, so I had my kids do a "Cajun Christmas." I chose a zydeco song, in French, which, translated, goes something like "My darling, my dear, you little flirt, nobody does it like you do." It had nothing to do with Christmas, but based on the amount of idiocy I've contended with, I surmised that nobody would notice.

I was ambitious in the choreography of the dance routine. It had many complicated parts, but under the threat of death and homework my thirty-one charges learned them meticulously, baring their teeth in a mandatory smile all the way. I'm exaggerating; I know they kind of enjoyed the rehearsals, the anticipation of performance and success. They know I would never let them fail. That's why they do what I ask, no matter how much they complain.

I had the children make their own costumes in class. All the boys and some of the girls were going to be alligators from the bayou and would dance with girls in red dresses with poinsettias in their hair. Christmas colors, red and green, get it? Meanwhile, a large, twinkling Christmas tree would sway in the background.

I gave Vanessa, lolloping and clumsy, the special task of introducing our festive fiasco. The line was, "Here come the good times, Cajun style!," which she said the first multitude of times as "Here come the good times, Asian style!" This caused me a lot of chagrin, thinking then that people would mistake our alligators for Godzillas. I tried to impress upon her the importance of word choice in this case, to which she suggested I assign another girl to the job. I declined, insisting nobody could do it as well as she could, if only this small detail could be perfected. She sighed and rehearsed, evolving into "Here come the good times, Haitian style!" and then to the correct "Cajun style!" under the mercy of our Maker.

During practices, the beams beneath the stage, well, I could see them buckling under the weight of 1,500 jumping pounds. I laughed to myself, imagining the scene of the entire stage being smashed, children cracking through the plastic floor so ungenerously afforded them, parents shrieking and knocking each other over in the path of rescue, Mr. Turner and his girlish look of terror—the one he gets whenever anyone mentions litigation. I laughed to myself, vowing to roll with the punches, to enjoy all catastrophes upon their arrival either in reality or in my imagination.

Reality, though, was a success! My class was the most attractive, most festive, most ambitious, most original, and noisiest. They were the most smiling, most intricate, most cooperative. They made me proud. They made themselves proud.

About fifteen of their parents attended. Some came up afterward, to congratulate them. I received no hellos or merry Christmases. I received no cards from parents and very few from the children. At 1:45 a posse came up to me and demanded angrily, "So, where's our presents?"

I have a silly job.

PART II

"There is no life I know
to compare with Pure Imagination.

Living there, you'll be free,
if you truly wish to be."

—Gene Wilder as Willy Wonka
in *Willy Wonka and the
Chocolate Factory*

January 6

The time machine! Really, an old refrigerator box covered with aluminum foil, with a flashing police car light rigged at the top and various knobs and keyboards screwed and glue-gunned on. Inside, a comfortable pillow for sitting and a flashlight attached to a curly phone cord. Maya helped me install a bookshelf inside the box with a power drill. She is such a quiet, good girl, the kind present teachers send to fetch coffee and future husbands will send to fetch beer. Of course, she loved driving the screws.

The idea: time travel through books.

I left the machine in the classroom, buckled and locked closed with lots of signs all over it: "Top secret!" "Under construction!" "No peeking, this means YOU!" "Danger! Highly radioactive!" and the like to build anticipation. The big question buzzing: Is it real? Does it really work?

A tricky question. I recollect clambering over laundry bags in the back of my parents' closet, eyes clamped closed, one hand groping, praying that I might enter C. S. Lewis's Narnia. Or, moving forward delicately, eyes closed once again, toward the mirror in our dining room in the hopes that I might go through like Alice managed in *Through the Looking Glass*. Alas, my head bumped the back of the closet, my fingers could not penetrate the glass. This did not negate that such adventures were possible, only that I was not among the lucky ones to be so enchanted.

"Yes, it really works," I offered, acting slightly perturbed that they would ever doubt me.

In the weeks before winter break, children from other classrooms have popped in to deliver messages or borrow things, and they stared bug-eyed. "Is it real? Does it really work?"

"Yes, of course," the children sniffed, now annoyed at the skepticism.

Then, the next biggest question: Who would be the first daring hero to risk his or her life in the contraption? In the interest of fairness, this seemed best left to chance, even at the risk that some terrible realist like B. B. was chosen, who I imagined would announce, "It's nothing but a box full of books! It's a fake!"

It turned out that JoEllen was chosen. We sent her off with much fanfare, with me pressing buttons and turning knobs feverishly, double-checking for accuracy that the medieval period was properly set, making her promise that her mother would not sue me should something . . . unexpected . . . occur.

"Like what?" asked JoEllen.

"Being eaten," I ventured.

"Oooooh!" The class crooned enviously.

"Yes, I hear that dragons possibly existed," I began, "though people may have believed that due to the inexplicable presence of dinosaur remnants found during the period. Still, if you'd rather give up your spot . . ."

"I'll risk it," JoEllen said quickly.

"You're on school time," I reminded her. "In the event that you return in one piece, I expect a full report on what you saw."

In she went. The doors closed. On went the police car light. "Back to work." Silent reading time.

In a half-hour, I retrieved her. She came out, breathless. "What did you see?" Everybody wanted to know. JoEllen paused. For thought? for effect? I'll never know.

"A joust."

"A what?"

"Two guys. Fighting on horses. Their armor clanging as they rode. Even the horses wore armor on their heads. The guys carried two big sticks. Everyone was watching and cheering, like a sport. One of the guys died, ran through with a stick . . ."

The class was impressed. "Write it in your journal before you forget," I suggested. "Who's next?"

For the rest of the day, the kids took turns in the time machine. So far, nobody has said, "It's just a box full of books."

After school, I shut the lights to leave and saw the machine with its red light still carouseling around. "Their armor clanging as they rode," I remembered. The words, the detail, they seemed different from what JoEllen regularly produces. I couldn't help squinting suspiciously at the silver box before turning it off.

January 7

This whole week at school has been very good. I kept waiting for something bad to happen, but nothing did. The only kind of bad thing: It was snowing so beautifully outside, first snow kind of snow, powdery, glittering, ivory, the neighborhood was frosted and perfect. So I took all thirty-one kids outside, just around the square block, to see which trees were deciduous and which were coniferous. I told Ms. Coil that I was going, but she didn't mention it to anyone. We left from the side door and tried to re-enter from the front door, but it was locked. Mr. Turner happened to be near the door. Wow! He spazzed that we were outside. The liability! etc. He comes goose-stepping over to the door. His face was all crumpled, his forehead in a pulled seam.

"Here comes that faggot," Vanessa remarked upon seeing his approach.

"Don't insult faggots," I countered.

I got reprimanded but played dumb. Ha-ha! Sky's the limit, since I bet this will be my only year teaching.

Today was especially cool. I got my Happy Box back, for one thing. Some kid said he found it in a public park, under a bush. I gave him the five dollar reward. The other teachers said I shouldn't have given him squat, that he probably took it in the first place. Even if he did, I think he's learned a valuable lesson about extortion, and that deserves to be rewarded.

The other fab thing was that the Slick Boys rap group came and did a Just Say No assembly at our school today. They had huge amps and "hoochie girls" rubbing their crotches and oscillating. It was great, of course, but I couldn't help thinking that school assemblies sure have changed since I was a kid. They did all their hip-hop dancing and blabbing incoherently into the microphones. Music was blaring at a deafening volume, but hey, rock and roll! They brought kids onstage to dance as they performed. I tried to get my kids into it. I was in the aisle, getting kids to clap along and root for them or whatever, when one of the rapper guys brought me by the hand onstage. Wow, the kids went bananas to see a teacher with the Slick Boys.

A roar went up, so I totally kicked it and did my *Soul Train* thing like I do at home! My class was laughing so hard, to see me do the "Humpty Dumpty"! Zykrecia shouted, "Madame Esmé got the moves! She got it going on!" and hopped onstage with me. When they saw us enjoying ourselves, a lot of other kids followed. It was my dream come true, I was an R&B pedagogue. I was very happy. The other teachers were kind of shocked, but what the hell! You only live once—in Western culture anyway.

January 8

I read in Melanie's journal that her birthday came and went without a cake. She had to remind her mom that it was her birthday. So I got her a cupcake and a candle and gift-wrapped a little purse. I had her wait in the room after school, while I picked up her little sister outside. We had Melanie cover her eyes. When she uncovered them, the candle was lit. We sang "Happy Birthday" to her. She looked moved—kind of a weird thing to see in a ten-year-old—quiet, thoughtful, smiling. She said thank you very nicely, very sincerely. I was glad, because I think she understood that I did it because I care about her.

The kids are studying about Anne Frank. They ask a lot of questions about the concentration camps, but I don't tell them in any detail. They seemed to grasp the gravity of the history when I compared the Nazis to the Klan. In their private journals, there is a disproportionate number of references to the Klan, considering we live in the city. Zykrecia even wrote about a dream where the Klan was riding through the streets of her neighborhood on horses, clad in their white sheets. Maybe it's because some of the kids spent time down South, I don't know, but when I compared Nazis and white supremacists, an audible groan of recognition went up. I don't tell them about the gas chambers or cremations. If they want to learn more on their own, they're sure to unearth the terrible information, and I'll tell them at the end. But what's the point of desensitizing them or frightening them with depictions of bodies being plowed into mass graves, like the seventh-grade teacher is doing? They're still children, for God's sake!

They are quite interested and involved, asking questions like "Why?" and "How could people let it happen?" Some of them have been staying in from recess to listen to a recording of Otto Frank talking about his daughter's work. Valerie was weeping at her desk during free choice reading time. I looked over her shoulder and discovered she was making a "Holocaust word search," where you find words like "anti-Semite" and "Nazi" and "genocide." Fifth-grade response to the dramas of our century.

THE KIDS HAVE free choice reading time in the afternoon, usually twenty minutes. This week, though, the kids have been reading for forty-minute stretches, so intently, I could hear my own breathing. It was eerie. A teacher popped in for something and saw this. "My God," she said. "So quiet and involved! Must be the weather." But it's not the weather. I've worked so hard to get them to this place, harder than I've ever worked in my life, and now it seems they have arrived. I want to take credit for getting them there, and they can have the credit for being there. We worked together to achieve this; it's hard to explain, except that it's not the weather or the boy-girl ratio or luck or any other such bullshit. It's that I try and they're trying, that's the bottom line.

Let it be known that I had one really good week teaching at this school!

January 9

THE CUSTODIAN'S THOUGHTS

A lonely job this is, letters on their pin-hinges
    hung,
Crooked. The children have gone.
The posy on the desk is elliptical on its stem,
Kept after school, bent with remorse.
Look at the teacher, gathering her things to go,
Her hair severe, foreshadowing the ebb of her life's
    tide.
Dumb bitch! Someday I'll give her a grab,
That ought to respirate 'er, surrender up a
Dimple or a laugh, for my dustpan . . .
Tsk! Don't these kids do anything all day
But crumple and pick at their papers, chew
    gum?
Give me the chalk! I'd teach them a thing or two
About tattoos, music and brooms:
Things a man can use.

January 10

Read-aloud time is my favorite time. We are starting *King Matt the First* by Janusz Korczak. It has hundreds of pages. It could take the rest of the year! It's so good, about a country run by a little boy king. Korczak was a pediatrician who ran an orphanage in Warsaw. He wrote the book for his charges. Eventually they all perished in the Holocaust. It's a good follow-up to *Number the Stars* by Lois Lowry, about the Danish resistance, which they read over the winter break (I bought all thirty-one copies myself, but it was worth it). The kids love the book so far. Even if I read for forty minutes, they complain when it's time to stop. Every chapter ends with a bit of a cliff-hanger.

RUBEN HAS A crush on me, I think. When we gather near the lamp for read-aloud, he always sits right next to my legs. Sometimes he touches my calf gently. The girls die laughing.

"Ruben, you're invading my space," I remind him.

"Sorry," he says genuinely, "but they're so smooth."

More gales of laughter. Ruben reddens, smiles sheepishly.

I tutor him one day a week after school with a yo-yo. He can "walk the dog" and almost do "around the world" now!

January 11

Miss Clark is the special education teacher. She keeps a lot of charts with gold stars. She's blond and thin and gorgeous. She makes them brownies when they all master a multiplication table. Isn't that nice? The kids eat her alive.

She tried to do a whole class lesson on her own, to make it up to me for blowing off helping my class as much as she's supposed to. I was in the back of the room getting some paperwork done. "I'm invisible," I told them. "Treat Miss Clark like she's your home-room teacher."

Unfortunately, they did. They weren't paying good attention and defied her, even though she kept saying please. Then she said, "Now we're going to do the nine-times tables."

"What'll you give us?" asked Kirk.

My mouth dropped open. I put down my pen.

Even more shockingly, Miss Clark answered, "Stickers."

"What'll you get! What'll you *get*!" I roared, suddenly becoming visible. "You'll get an education, that's what you'll get! Which is more than you deserve, for the rotten way you've been treating Miss Clark! You aren't getting *stickers,* you aren't getting *brownies,* you aren't getting *please and thank you,* you're getting to work, and you'll work double the assignment that Miss Clark gives you, I'll be checking on it. Now, who else wants to *get* something?"

Nobody else did. I thought I'd hear a chorus of tongue-clucking, but I didn't hear a peep. Everyone got to work. A couple of kids even quietly apologized as they passed Miss Clark to go to lunch.

Alone together, Miss Clark wept dainty tears from her luxurious lashes. "I just want them to like me," she squeaked.

"It's not our job to be liked," I reminded her. "It's our job to help them be smart." Secretly, I thought, Who gives a rat's ass if they like us? Sometimes I can hardly stand them!

. . .

January 12

Billy Williams is just out of control with the whining and tongue-clucking. "You always giving us home-work, and you ain't never give us no free time in class! I hate you!"

"You can hate me all you want. That's your prerog-ative, your choice. But no matter how you feel about me, I will always love you." I mostly say this because I know it just drives them crazy.

Sure enough, this sends Billy into a tongue-clucking frenzy. He stands up behind his desk. "I hate you!" he roars.

"I'm sorry you're angry, but I still love you, and I won't allow you to fail."

"Dang! Dang! You always saying you love us. Well, your love mean nothing to me, woman!"

"Oooh, you breakin' her heart, Billy Williams," laughed Selena. We all laughed.

"You think it's so hard to be on your side of the desk," I told Billy, "but you sure make it hard from where I stand. I'm pretty sick of it. How about you see

how hard you make it for me? You teach tomorrow."
The class went up for grabs.

"Shiiiiiit! That your job! I ain't doing it!"

I put up a thumb for attention. All was quiet. "Here's the deal. Teach tomorrow or be suspended for swearing, arguing, and not doing your work. Take your pick. Or rather, pick which one your mother would prefer when I call her about your decision tonight."

Billy looked like he would kill me.

January 13

"Would Mr. Williams please pick up his students." I got ahold of the intercom. Ms. Coil was made privy to the disciplinary action. The morning bell had rung. The class waited outside, delighted, in a perfect line. Billy was hiding in the boy's room. I told his mom the night before not to let him say he was too sick to come to school today. I waited for him. Finally, he emerged.

"You really gonna make me do this?"

"Just for a day."

"All day? You crazy!"

"No, I'm Billy." I took off his jacket and headphones and put them on. He's as big as me, so they fit. I put one of my boyfriend Jim's ties around his neck. "Got any gum, brother-man?" He didn't think my imitation was funny.

The rest of the class did.

I handed him the Trouble Basket.

"I ain't doing this!"

"Then you'll have more troubles than this one basket can carry," I threatened. "Don't forget to say 'Good morning.'"

Billy tried to take attendance. "There's some boys still out in the coat room," I heard Selena point out. I was having fun, hanging out in there with B. B. and Kirk.

"Come out of there!" Billy stuck his head in. "How I'm 'posed to take attendance! Damn!" B. B. and Kirk, realizing the consequences that Billy would deliver after school should they not cooperate, reluctantly went to their seats. I moseyed.

"Come on! Or I'll give you five dictionary definitions to copy!" Billy warned me.

"Dang, man, don't have a baby! I'll git there when I git there, and if that ain't good enough for you, well, ain't that too bad!" I leered.

Billy maintained his character, looking slightly saddened, but ignored me. Some smart girls offered to help him with the lunch count. He got everybody lined up for art in the room across the hall. He let them enter, then proceeded himself.

"Where do you think you're going?" I stopped him. "Do you see me go to art? You have lesson plans to prepare. Lucky for you, it's a double period."

We went to the teacher's lounge. I brought books with various science experiments in them. Of course, he liked some exciting ones, but I reminded him that there weren't many materials at his disposal. He finally decided on paper airplanes. He had to choose which pages to make handouts from. He ran the copy machine. Then he took notes for background knowledge. I reminded him to use the washroom before picking up the children, that it would be his only chance in the day.

Billy picked up the class and took them to the washroom. By now the novelty of the situation was on the wane, and the children were in full form. Two girls started smacking each other.

"Cut it out!" Billy broke it up. They went back at it. "Don't make me suspend y'all!"

"*You* can't suspend us, Billy Williams."

"That's *Madame* Billy Williams today," he corrected, "and I believe I *can*."

The girls turned to me for reassurance. "What cha'll lookin' at me fo'? Like what you see?" I flashed them my winning Williams smile. The girls looked at me, then Billy, laughed nervously, and fell into line.

Walking back, I followed about six feet behind the rest of the class, like Billy does.

"Come on, yo' highness!" Billy imitated.

"Dang! Dang! Always raggin' on me!" I railed.

"Five definitions."

"You hate me!" I clenched my fists. "You hate me 'cause I'm black!"

"I love you," he retorted, "but I don't always love the choices that you make."

When we returned to the classroom, Billy added a letter *W* to the "h-o-m-e" that was already spelled out on the board from yesterday. If it spells "homework" on Friday, that's what they get. The kids howled.

"That's for fightin' and arguin' in the hall. Ya'll know better." The kids continued to complain noisily. "Next time, you'll make a better choice," he consoled. I had to hand it to him.

"Now, Mr. Williams and elephants never forget," he sing-songed, using one of my pet phrases. "Test time."

"Oooh!" The kids complained, none louder than me.

"We ain't got to do what the teacher says! He ain't the boss of us!" I tried to incite mutiny, as Billy does whenever a test is mentioned. "He ain't said nothin' about no test!"

"Says here on the board "t-e-s-t," which I believe spells test, and "T-h-u-r-s-d-a-y," which I believe spells today, so get out your pencils, which should already be as sharp as I know your answers will be."

I nearly fainted. For a kid who doesn't do what I say, he sure hears what I say.

"Wait! Is Madame Esmé taking Billy's test?" Selena queried. Billy looked at me.

"Of course," I came out of character for a moment to announce, "I'll take it, as Billy would."

Billy didn't look very comfortable. "Did you study?" he asked as he handed me the test.

"Ya'll didn't say nothin' 'bout no test! Dang!"

Billy rolled his eyes.

Throughout the test, I made a point of leaning over to see Ruben's answers, tossing paper at kids' heads for their attention, and sighing audibly with frustration. Billy sent me a mixed assortment of disapproving looks. Finally, I turned in a C test, figuring that was at least a full grade above his average.

Billy took the children to lunch. I bought him a teacher's lunch, and he ate with me in the teacher's lounge. He looked funny, sitting with all the men and women in his T-shirt and tie.

"So you're the teacher today, huh!" one of the teachers quipped.

"Yes'm," he muttered.

"Doing a fabulous job, too," I added.

Billy smiled into his sloppy joe.

After lunch Billy launched into his paper airplane

lesson. While he was beginning his explanation, Mr. Turner walked in. Billy was poised with a sample airplane, and I was slouched down at his desk.

"I didn't do it!" I yelled when Mr. Turner entered. The class laughed.

"Raise your hand if you have something to share," Mr. Williams corrected patiently.

Mr. Turner looked at us, one, then the other, and walked out. At the end of the day, Ms. Coil told me he came back to the office and said, "Something's going on in Cordell's room, but I'm not sure I want to know what it is."

I let Mr. Williams off the hook at the last period of the day, assigning a composition, "The Day Billy Williams Was Our Teacher." I wrote a composition during the period, too, "The Day Madame Esmé Was Billy Williams." At the end of the day, I read it to the class: How I had forgotten how hard it is not to chew gum, how uncomfortable the seats were, what a pain it is to have to go to the washroom with the class when you don't even have to *go,* how scary it is when you forget to study, how easy it is to feel stupid even if you're smart. I let Billy have my composition, and he took the rest of them home to grade. I looked at the one on top, by Zykrecia.

"I cant beleave she rilly did it. She said she would and she did. Billy Williams was our teacher today. He couldant really control us but other than that he did a good job. He always givin trouble well now he got some, I think he learnt a good lessin. Madam was actin just like Billy. It made me feel good that she re-members what it like. She ast me for gum but I didint have any. Maybe Ill be real bad so I can be teacher next."

After school I complimented Billy on a job well done, and that I thought he would be a fine teacher someday, if that's what he chose.

"Ain't choosin' it," he grumbled, smiling. "Too hard."

I gave Billy my old harmonica from when I was eleven and told him I'd teach him to play it, if he still wanted me for a teacher.

Note to self: Give Zykrecia some help on contractions.

• • •

January 18

"When are you going to fix up your room so I can show it to people?' asks Ms. Coil.

"Just as soon as you tell me what on earth you mean," I replied.

"No time right now."

"You took the time to insult me, surely you can take a moment to back it up."

She came up to my room. "I'm just trying to give you teachers constructive criticism. I don't know why everyone is getting so defensive," she worried aloud.

"Oh?"

"You've actually responded in a much more professional manner," she continued cheerfully. "Most of the teachers just told me to fuck off."

"That's what happens when you ask people who are giving a hundred and one percent of themselves to give one hundred and two," I observed. "I'm interested in the specifics of your constructive criticism. I promise I won't tell you to fuck off, at least, not out loud. So fire away!"

"Well!" Her whole face lit up with the joy of opportunity. "Every time I come in here, I think, your art center's marker tray should be on the right side, not the left. You see!" I didn't.

"Okay. Right, not left. Anything else?"

"Yes. All these papers. You have them hanging so low. Why don't you hang them high? Over the windows, see?" She was whirling around like Kay Thompson in Paris in *Funny Face*.

"I see, but I don't think the children, averaging about four and a half feet tall, will. If it's all the same to you, I'd like to keep the best work at kids' eye level."

"Oh-kaaaaaaay." She was unconvinced.

"Anything else?"

"The main thing," she said, "is this poster, on this section of wall. I think you should move it to this section," four feet over.

"I like the poster where it is."

She took the poster down and rehung it where she preferred.

"I liked the poster where it was," I reiterated, "and if you'll excuse my saying so, I'm the one who is in this room between six and ten hours every day."

"It's still your room!" Ms. Coil exclaimed, surprised. Then she left.

It made me sick, seeing my poster hanging there.

Note to self: Must get Ms. Coil.

January 19

Today, went into Ms. Coil's office. She was sitting at her desk, filling something out. Got the plant off of her desk. Put it on her bookshelf. She stared at me.

"It's still your office," I said and left.

January 20

Had a field trip to the Sulzer Regional Library this past week. Seven parents said they'd help me chaperone. None showed up. I finally found two parents from other classrooms who were dropping off their children. They said they'd help if I bought them lunch.

At the morning teacher's meeting, Mr. Turner said teachers "must work harder to help the children achieve their dreams and expirations." I started laughing so hard, Ms. Coil had to pinch my leg under the table to get me to stop. I mean, I guess that's why she was pinching me.

February 1

Well, they stabbed the substitute today. In the back, with a pencil. The paramedics said it was only a flesh wound. She didn't press any charges, she just went home.

"Who did it!" Mr. Turner howled at them. They were silent. Who in their right mind would say anything? He stomped out.

I sat behind my desk and looked at them. They were sitting very nicely. The mood in the room was somewhat pleasant. I had been gone only twenty minutes. Mr. Turner had called me out to troubleshoot some computer problem and had called in a substitute who was on a break from filling in for another teacher. When I came back, this woman was gone. In twenty minutes, had they really managed to stab someone?

"Would anyone tell me . . . why?" I asked, genuinely curious.

"It your fault," Vanessa grinned.

"My fault!" I laughed incredulously.

"Yes," explained Selena. "You're the one who is always telling us, 'Treat people the way you would like to be treated.' Well, she told Donna she was fat, and she told Vanessa she was stupid. She ain't treated us like we like to be treated. So . . ." Her "so" trailed off by means of explanation.

"I see." I mashed down the smile that I felt humming behind my lips. "But I wonder . . . Did you treat her as she would like to be treated? When you stabbed her in the back?"

"With a pencil," offered Kirk.

"Yes, thank you, Kirk, with a pencil."

"She didn't die," Vanessa reminded me.

"No, she didn't. You only wounded her. You didn't kill her. Very good." I tried to be encouraging. "But there seems to be some misunderstanding. You see, you must treat people as you would like to be treated even in the event that they are ignorant and don't treat you as you would like to be treated. That's the tricky part. You must follow the Golden Rule even if you think they are stupid. Even if they don't follow the

Golden Rule, you don't bring yourselves down to their level."

The children now hung their heads.

"I'm sorry. I should have explained it more clearly. Perhaps it is my fault," I suggested. A heavy silence hung.

"We'll do better next time," Vanessa called out brightly.

"Yeah! We get it now!" said Kirk. "We're sorry."

"Don't say you're sorry to me," I said. "I'm not the one with a pencil stuck in my back."

The children laughed at this, reminisced briefly about the humor in seeing a pencil in someone's back, and began working industriously from their T.T.W.E. texts. From behind my desk, I stared at them, wondering whether to be afraid. Didn't Malcolm X say something like, "Only those who do not understand us have reason to fear"?

At the end of the period, I jokingly said, "May I assign homework, or will I then need to watch my back?"

"Not you, Madame Esmé," said Selena.

That made me feel a little better.

February 7

We just finished a unit about Native Americans. I thought it was very successful. We studied several tribes in depth, and I paid a man from the Native American Education Service to come in and give a presentation about the parallels between Native and African Americans toward the building of our nation. He brought in lots of unusual artifacts, too.

To culminate the unit we had a powwow. We painted our faces and made headdresses according to research and learned as authentic a rain dance as we could find. Asha's mother helped make her a really nice Native American–style vest for the occasion. It made me feel good, like Asha was interested enough to tell her mom what she was learning, and Asha's mom was interested enough to get involved.

We had a naming ceremony, in which we went in a circle, and someone would volunteer to give that person a name that capitalized on some positive feature. It was a very thoughtful time. JoEllen was given "Girl of Many Questions." Donna was given "Girl with Cheeks Like Smiling Chipmunk." Ozzie was "Boy Who

Draws Like Crazy." Monique was "Hair That Flows Like Water." I was pleased that the children stayed encouraging in the names they gave. I wrote out each name as it was decided upon on a badge for the student to wear. Then the children named me "Woman With Many Children."

They wore their costumes down to lunch. They were very quiet in the hall. Ms. Coil commented on this. "Why aren't you making noise, like wild Indians?"

Tobias, line captain, looked disdainful. "We're Iroquois, not Comanche," he said by way of explanation. Hearing him say that was like getting to give a perfect score on a test. I knew he got it.

Like every successful day, it seems, it ended by getting called into the office.

"I 'did' Native Americans when I taught kindergarten," boasted Ms. Coil.

"That's nice."

"I had them dress up, too. Don't you think fifth grade is kind of old for dress-up?"

"They were comfortable enough," I shrugged.

"I notice by your lesson plans you didn't quiz them

after each tribe. Maybe next time, Woman With Many Children." She read my badge.

"Yeah, maybe, Big Chief Micromanager."

Nobody around here seems to like my brand of humor.

February 12

Draggy things this week: Mr. Turner looking at my breasts. Takes all the joy out of wearing a leotard. Proceeded to ask me to do a schoolwide promotion of milk.

February 15

I finished typing a pretty terrific newsletter for our classroom. The kids wrote great articles. Gave it to the lesser of two evils, Ms. Coil, not out of love, purely to cover my ass in case of an insane parent. I guess she got excited, though, and showed Mr. Turner. He started out complimentary but quickly annoyed me, saying that he felt "hurt" that I didn't put one in his mailbox. I acted surprised, like I must have accidentally shoved it in the wrong box in my haste. I felt stupid telling such a meaningless lie, but I felt it more polite than saying, "I tend not to share things unnecessarily with those I despise." He reminded me that I must show him parent communications before I send them out, or he will have to write me up. Furthermore, he wished that I wouldn't put so much energy into my classroom and more into the whole school.

I said I thought I did do a lot. I brought up the Connie Porter assembly. He said that was nice, but it's a new marking period now, and what had I done? I brought up the fact that I volunteered to sponsor two after-school extracurricular programs. He said he wanted me to work on the school paper; that is, invent a school paper. I said it would be my pleasure, to the extent that it doesn't interfere with helping the thirty-one children in my charge.

"I hired you to help out around the whole school."

"I think you ask a lot of a first-year teacher," I answered flatly.

Later that same day, he called me into his office. He had a computer printout of the guidelines of the school social committee, which I unfortunately chair. I had signed the bottom "Madame Esmé," which was the source of conflict, but he doesn't tell me this right away. He just looks grumpy and closes the door to his office, which, from precedent, I translate to be the overture to an unprofessional action. So I say, "Mr. Turner, please open the door or allow me to have another teacher present."

"That's not necessary," he says.

I say, "I feel it is," and get up and open the door myself.

He says, "No, it's not," and gets up and slams the door. I felt intimidated and weirded out.

Then he lays the "Madame" thing on me. "I thought we had this settled. I'll put it in writing that I don't want any correspondence to leave this school with you signing your name 'Madame.' It's enough I let the children call you Mrs. Esmé!"

Lets the children! "I am not discussing this with you in this way any further." I got up and moved to the door.

When I had one foot in and one foot out, he yelled, "If you leave when I AM SPEAKING TO YOU, THEN

YOU ARE DEFIANT! I'll have you down for DEFI-ANCE!" His eyes were all big and flashy.

Standing in the threshold of his office, time seemed to slow down as I considered his observation and subsequent threat. Being a teacher, my initial response was the desire to compliment him on his acquisition of such a challenging daily word as "defiance." Bravo! Then I felt sobered, heavy, and sad, and a part of me also felt very, very tired, of the sick-and-tired variety. *This is one of those "if . . . then," puzzles,* I thought. *The kids will pay in the long run if I get canned. Stick your nose in his ass like he wants. Don't win the battle. Win the war.*

I turned around and re-entered his office. I said, "Here!" and scratched out the word *madame* on the printout so hard, right under his nose, until the pen scratched through the paper and I could feel it grinding into his blotter. I was really mad. Then I walked back to my classroom and had a tantrum, throwing some erasers and chalk and crying. I changed my mind about not saying what I think. If you let people walk over you while you're young, you should get used to wearing feet marks across your face for the rest of your life. So I packed my school bag and started downstairs.

"Where are you going?" I was intercepted by Ms. Federman.

"I'm going to tell Mr. Turner that I am going to grow a dick so he can suck it!" I explained gleefully.

"I figured," she sighed. "Stop in my room first." It seemed Mr. Turner called her in and told her what happened, asked her opinion. I like Ms. Federman, but I still felt Mr. Turner was unprofessional to do that. A principal is not supposed to talk about problematic teachers with other teachers.

I felt sheepish, crying in Ms. Federman's room. I knew I must seem stubborn and smug. "Compromise is fine for people who aren't as right as me." I tried to laugh, but it was forced, because in reality I am stubborn and smug.

Ms. Federman didn't laugh. She is also stubborn and smug. And expert. She has a slightly South-side affect, a kind of nasal Alabama twang that is funny on a middle-aged Jewish woman. She takes these wonderful intimidating deep breaths, like a bull preparing to charge, when one of her students is about to get back twice the amount of trouble he gave to her. She has antagonized some first-year teachers, too, suggesting to Mrs. Rae that she might go to jail if she didn't follow the state mandate of saying the "Pledge of Allegiance" every morning. At the same time, she asks the new teachers for ideas, and uses them. She shares. She does what she has to, to continue her twenty-some years of teaching.

God! Twenty years of teaching. I can't imagine.

"Why are you doing this?" she asked me.

"I can't change who I am just because someone tells me to!" I started to rail. "If he could give me a real reason . . ."

"Oh, *that*," she scoffed. "I know why you do *that*. Nobody would hang on to that 'Madame' shtick unless they were really crazy. Like you said, you can't change that. I meant, why are you teaching?"

"Lack of foresight?"

She smiled but didn't laugh at my half-joke.

"What would happen to the kids if you left?"

"They'd be taught by somebody else."

"It wouldn't be you."

"And yet, the earth would somehow continue to revolve around the sun."

"Every school has its problems."

"Yeah, well, I want to trade my problems in for a different set. Look, Ms. Federman, I don't mean to be rude, but this is ridiculous. I can't win here."

"You've already won. You're right in what you're doing with the kids. What else do you want to win?" She looked at me with a sad smile, the smile of a single-parent teaching veteran who has eaten more shit than fits in all the septic systems in Chicago. Maybe Ms. Federman just wants me around for entertainment value, to say the things she can't say, since she's got that beautiful daughter who depends on her. Not everybody's in a position to flip the bird to administration. "Compromise isn't always something you do for somebody else. Save your job for yourself. If you want to leave, wait for the big fight."

"I don't want to fight anymore."

"Ha! You call that a fight? You wait until you've been teaching in the city awhile. See if you can stay here after you come up against *the* fight. The fight that will prove Mr. Turner's just the captain of a sinking ship. The fight that's bigger than two people in a room. It's a fight that you can't win even though you're right, because you can't win it all by yourself."

I tried to pout, but I grew too curious. "What's the fight about?" I had to know.

She just shook her head, smiling.

She got me. The plea for selfishness. But even more, the mysterious Bigger Fight. I am American, after all. I saw *The Empire Strikes Back*. What sort of Jedi would I be if I don't really face the Dark Side? Mr. Turner may be Vader, but is there an enemy that remains to be revealed, like that bossy old wrinkled guy who told Vader what to do?

Somehow, Ms. Federman talked me out of quitting. In some ways, I wished she hadn't.

February 21

I was really miserable, but then I thought, *Hey, I'll be union representative! Then he'll leave me alone!* I asked our current representative, who is about a year away from retiring, if she wanted to be relieved. She said no, but I ended up telling her what happened. She thought it was all a big power play because I'm a rookie. She said next time just tell him I spoke to her. I asked, "Is it being defiant if I say, 'Please don't tell me to do extra things, ask me, and I can only do what I know is realistic for me to be able to do'?" She said no, it isn't, and to use the word *grievance* if he keeps hassling me with extra responsibilities or tries to close the door. I felt better. I didn't see Mr. Turner all that Thursday.

Then Friday I got called out of the computer lab, where I was helping to supervise my class. Mr. Turner was in the hall. He said, "I want the milk project information back." I was delighted.

We went to my classroom, where I had filed the milk project garbage, and we were alone. I didn't bother to turn on the lights, because I knew where to look. I got the papers and turned around, almost slamming into Mr. Turner. He was standing right behind me. He looked all tense and pinched and he had his fists clenched, consciously or unconsciously, God knows. Once again I felt intimidated, I realized, as the hairs on my neck began to prickle.

"Cordell, did you call the union?"

"No," I snapped, "but thanks for asking."

That last remark made absolutely no sense, I realize. I must have said it to conceal my real question: "So what if I did?"

Maybe I'm blowing this out of proportion, but I am really getting depressed and annoyed. Other teachers are getting mad at me.

"Don't make him angry—you know he'll just take it out on us."

"Stop being so confrontational, you're bringing down morale."

"You should have been born a man. You've got balls of steel."

I don't understand my life right now.

February 28

I make the kids do so much math, an hour and a half straight every day. Is it because I was so bad at it, I want them to be good? They were having trouble multiplying double digits. It is tricky, how you're supposed to move stuff around as you bring it down to add. So we got out huge pieces of butcher paper and wrote problems on them, and I masking-taped them to the floor. Then I put on "Mu-Cha-Cha" from *Bells Are Ringing*. (They already know how to cha-cha. I taught them a while ago.) I started dancing on the butcher paper, making my feet do the math. Forward, multiply the ones. Back, bring it down. Side, the ones column by the tens. Back, down and over. Side, multiply the tens by the ones. Back, extra step, and over. On and on. Soon, all the kids were dancing on problems. Then we did some multiplication at our desks. "Pretend your pencils are your feet," I instructed as the music played.

Much improved.

Got a nice letter from Tobias. "Thank you for teaching us the distributive cha-cha. It really help me. P.S. The cha-cha and distributive math are sort of fun."

March 3

My boyfriend, Jim, has so many conspiracy theories. I think he gives people too much credit. I so rarely meet a single person who is very well organized, or with any direction. What are the chances of meeting a whole group?

But then, when I'm sitting at these teacher's meetings, I think maybe Jim is right. All these people conspiring to make children's days as boring and meaningless as possible. All the meetings are variations on a theme: How can we all be the same and get the children to do likewise? On any given agenda: lines and keeping children in them, the proliferation of talking and how to stop it, textbooks and state goals, are all the children learning what everyone else is learning?

Today, Mr. Turner explained that progress is being made in regard to receiving funds from the Jordan Foundation, run by Michael Jordan's mother, so from now on teachers are to always uphold highest in their teaching the "Jordan Rules," and the standards of excellence should be in accordance with the standards set by the Jordans.

After the meeting, I approached Mr. Turner, and asked him if the Michael Jordan approach to pedagogy was in any way congruous with Mickey Mantle's approach to pedagogy. He became very angry and said he didn't care what my philosophy was, just try to do what he asks for a change.

I am very excited. Tomorrow I get to teach the children how to slam dunk!

March 6
- -

The children did good visual and oral reports about different vertebrates. Melanie did her report about the rat. In the center she had glued on specimens, clearly labeled RAT POO DROPPINGS. Her presentation, though not particularly scholarly, was definitely pragmatic. "Take care to tuck in the sides of your blankets, or they'll climb up on to your bed, it's really awful."

I read them "The Pudding Like the Night on the Sea" from *The Stories Julian Tells,* in which a father threatens his sons with a whipping and a beating, only to have them whip cream and beat eggs to make a pudding for their mother. I used different voices for the different characters. They loved it. They laughed so hard, some of them were wheezing to catch their breath. I laughed, too. It felt so good. I thought: *This is what it's all been for, this moment of having my own classroom, laughing together.*

March 13

I am really liking how we are doing reading now. I spent a fortune on multiple copies of children's books, about eight per title. The kids are arranged in groups, and each child is assigned a role: The "discussion director" makes up questions about the book, the "literary luminary" reads aloud notable parts, the "language lover" defines what she determines to be the hardest words in the section, the "practical predictor" predicts what will happen next, and finally the "process checker" sums it up, keeps track of everyone's participation, and decides how many pages they must read that night. They keep notebooks documenting their work.

Within twenty minutes, each group has a reading meeting with each person doing his or her job. They take turns with a "talking stone" from a collection of beautiful minerals I have; only the person in the group holding the stone may speak. So far nobody has thrown a stone at anyone else. In fact, the children strive to be efficient so their group can have first pick from the minerals the next day.

They are given a test date, and it is their responsibility to have the book completed by that day. Each group is responsible for a presentation—a diorama, time line, rap, dramatic scene, whatever—that relates to the book but doesn't give away the ending. Each child takes an individual comprehension test for the book. The groups present their projects the following day. The day after that, we rotate the books. It downplays ability grouping and helps with self-esteem.

I also bought whole classroom sets of books, like *The Twenty-One Balloons* by William Pène Du Bois. I will read the first chapter aloud, and then they will complete it over the vacation break. Their caretakers sign permission slips before I let any student borrow anything from me. I plan on reading one whole book aloud while the children follow along with their own copies, so they can see words as they are spoken. Probably *The Wish Giver* by Bill Brittain. We still have daily read-alouds and Free Reading Time, too. I believe exposure to print is the key to reading achievement. So far, it has also been the key to reading enthusiasm. We are having a good time and reading by the pile!

March 22

We are working on a felt quilt, with each patch featuring a state flower. All the kids have to be able to locate all fifty states to pass the fifth grade, says me. The patches are going very nicely. I taught those who didn't already know how to thread needles and sew. The boys resisted, but I pointed out there might not always be a woman around to mend their socks. They rescinded. Ashworth's stitches are so even. I told his mom he was great at sewing. She said it must be in the blood: His grandfather was a tailor.

Vanessa, Donna, Melanie, and Latoya composed a "quilted poem." They explained that each put in one line, and then in the last line they brought all the pieces together. It's called "Quilting":

Quilting makes us feel like old women in rocking chairs,
Old men telling stories to their grandsons.

It feels so good to sew,
You go in and out and in and out,
You feel like the world's going around in circles.

March 24

B. B. and his little sister Leesha slept over at my apartment while their mom got a restraining order for the man of the house, who shot her once in the arm. She had been hesitating because she wanted the kids to be somewhere else when he found out, or he might take it out on them. I worried about keeping them overnight, if she'd lie and say I did something sick to get money from me. *I could ruin my whole career by doing this,* I thought. But then I thought, *How can I not do it? What if something happens to them tonight? How will I live with myself?* So I told B. B.'s mom okay. I didn't tell the administration, because I knew they'd get all noodle-kneed about possible litigations.

Once they were here, it was no big deal. We ordered a pepperoni pizza. Leesha had a bubble bath. B. B. brought his recorder and played a song for me. I read them some stories. Made eggs for breakfast. They were completely well mannered.

I told the school counselor the next day, just to cover my behind, in case B. B.'s mom got any bright ideas. The counselor cried and shook my hand. Most importantly, she said she wouldn't tell Mr. Turner.

March 28

At conflict resolution meeting, Zykrecia confronted Kyle.

"I didn't like it when you said you were going to take me doggy style. It made me feel angry and upset." The class, of course, roared, but collected themselves so rapidly, I did not even need to settle them down. I was proud of them, controlling themselves.

"I never said that!" said Kyle. Lying, but again I didn't participate. Selena broke in.

"It doesn't matter what you think you did," she articulated. "It matters what Zykrecia thinks you did. Use the information to change what you do in the future."

I was floored.

"What do you want in the future?" mediated Rochelle.

"I guess I just don't want you to say anything at all to me in the future. Don't speak to me."

The class looked at Kyle. His face was pained, devastated. Denial, his exit door, had been blocked off. He looked bloodless, shocked, leaning forward on his knuckles. The class waited.

"In the future, I won't speak to you," he squeaked. His face contorted with a certain shame, his mouth pulled tight in agony. It was profound. I held back, observed.

"Conflict solved?" Rochelle asked.

"If he does what he said, it is," said Zykrecia.

The class clapped. Then Zowela said, "I have a comment." She was recognized. "That must have been embarrassing for Zykrecia to say in front of everyone. I applaud her for saying it." All the girls clapped again. Poor Kyle looked shot. I thought of interjecting something in his defense; perhaps he didn't know. But really, there's no defense. And now he knows.

Kids were keeping their distance. They let him cry at his desk without interfering. He was angry. He said he was mad at me. I couldn't think why. Then I thought, *He's mad because I let this happen to him. He's hurting. He's hurting, but he's going to be accountable now.*

Kyle cried a lot today.

March 29

We went on a field trip to the Historical Society. Sluggish, friendly old white man with a hearing aid was our tour guide. My kids asked great questions, nodding in recognition at certain information. It's refreshing to see them in an out-of-school context, knowing stuff. Funny to hear them, too. Sometimes they parrot my phrases, my syntax. When the tour guide said, "These bullets from the American Revolution are made of lead," Valerie raised her hand and enunciated, à la Madame, "Doesn't it stand to *reason,* then, that King George would choose to tax lead?"

Also, when B. B. was getting out of line, Melanie leaned over with a warning index finger, "Is that *wise*?"

My girlfriend Lucy went with me, thank God. The

parents so rarely come to help. Lucy got a hankering for the kids' potato chips at lunch, so she said, "I'm Queen George, and I'm giving you a potato chip tax, five per table." She collected.

March 30

A lot of stupid stuff has happened, but I'm getting a better sense of humor about it. Here's something really weird:

As I was leaving the school at 4:30, Ms. Coil said, "Do you have to go home right away?"

To which I replied, "Why?"

"I need some help moving furniture at my house."

Well, I started to laugh, because I thought she couldn't be serious. I moved closer, in case I had misheard her.

"Can you?"

"I have to meet my friend in an hour," I lied.

"I'll have you back by then."

Oh, shit, roped into another one. What else is new. So I got into her fancy car. "This would be my *downtown* apartment," she begins and goes on to explain how this apartment is just for writing her *doctorate,* having the necessary *privacy* to do so, *away* from her *husband.*

"Virginia Woolf would be proud of you," I said, trying to be polite. "Do you like to write?"

"I like to cut and paste from the works of others," she explained flatly, without the humor that should have accompanied such a statement. She continued, rather indignantly, "My form of creativity is not considered a valid way of writing in my doctoral program; I could lose my chance at this degree, and I've come too far, too far. So I'll just have to force myself to create their way."

Poor plagiarist! "Must be hard on you," I sighed.

"Do you know that the doctor Martin Luther King cut and pasted?"

"Did 'the doctor,' indeed?"

"You see, it's not a sign of lacking."

"Not at all. You're like . . . a rapper. A sampler of sorts, taking bits and pieces to create your own. Is that what you're trying to say?"

"Well, not like a *rapper,*" she qualified. Of course

not. Rappers, what was I thinking? This woman has a degree. Pish-*posh!*

Anyway, I didn't say much more the whole ride. She was talking, overflowing with personal information: her marriage, her children, her education, how she recently failed a test for the first time, her dreams, her feelings about her work. *Why is she putting herself in such a vulnerable position?* I wondered. *Why is she sharing all this with me?* I listened closely for clues. I still couldn't fathom that she actually expected me, at hardly over a hundred pounds, to move furniture. I figured there was something she needed to say to me that she felt too weird saying directly, so she concocted this bizarre front.

I went to her high-rise building, and her apartment, sparsely decorated with tasteful, expensive furniture. Any item of brand-name fame was duly noted, and pricey pieces were tagged in detail. Of course, I was not impressed. Who am I, the insurance man? But I was polite. She came to some big photographic portrait of a little girl, modern, nondescript, overlaid in blue. "Not many people have art like this," she said. I didn't know what she meant, so I just posed like I was scrutinizing it. "It spoke to me, though. Not many people would have this kind of art, *black* art." The little girl was black.

"What do you want moved?" I cut to the chase.

It was a glass table with movable metal legs. "Does it look better here . . . or here?" She moved the legs, literally, a distance of three inches. I just stared, so she did it again. "Here . . . or here?"

"It looks the same to me."

"Look closer. Here . . . or here?"

"Come on, Ms. Coil, you've seen my classroom. You know I don't have that kind of attention to detail." I forced a laugh.

"Here, you try moving it. Move it from the legs, under here. Let me see."

So I was under the table on my knees, moving the table legs a distance of three inches, back and forth, back and forth, back and forth, and backandforth—I mean, a lot of times, way too many times for someone to move something within a three-inch radius, and there was just no end in sight. The thought occured to me: *Nobody in the whole world knows where*

I am, and Coil is acting kind of crazy. She could kill me, blow my brains out right under this table. Maybe the last thing I'll do in this life is move Coil's fucking table backandforthandbackandforthandbackandforth-and . . .

I stood up. "Looks fine," I said. "Now I've got to go back. Now."

"Are you sure it looks right?"

"Yes."

"What about these pictures?" They were pictures of her daughter. "Like this or this? This . . . or this?"

"Just put them where you can see them well," I said, "if they're of your family."

Somehow, under the mercy of God, we left. When we neared my apartment, she said, "Are you staying at the school?"

I saw no need to show my whole hand. A bluff was in order. "I'm undecided," I answered. "Depends on whether I'm offered a job at another school."

"And what are you going to do about the 'Madame' thing? Mr. Turner really has a problem with it."

Jackpot.

"It'd just be a shame if you lost your job over it."

"Well, if he chooses not to retain me over something so minor, I'll be just fine, and I think we all know whose loss it'll be." I smiled over my shoulder as I stepped out of the car. "And you can tell him I said so, when he asks you how it went."

Very weird, surreal, inappropriate. I told Mrs. Rae, who does a mean Ms. Coil imitation. She laughed uproariously, teasing. "She has a crush on you!"

Feh! Well, if Coil thinks we've bonded, she's got another thing coming. I'm not buddy-buddy with show-offs having midlife crises.

April 1

Mr. Turner came into my room yesterday when I was alone, around 4:30.

"What do you want?" I asked.

"I'm here for us to have a casual conversation. We can have a casual conversation, can't we?"

Now, I haven't had too many casual conversations begin like that. I gave him a fishy look, I think.

"Have a seat then, Mr. Casual."

He put on a big phoney smile and sat in one of

those hard plastic chairs next to my desk, where the bad boys who need a heart-to-heart usually sit.

"Where do you plan to be next year?" opens Mr. Casual.

"Mmmm . . . haven't given it much thought." I tilted my head and looked diagonally, like a cow chewing cud who hears a bell ringing; I really thought of that and tried to imitate the bovine gesture. It was the only thing that occured to me that would keep me from giving him a juicy Bronx cheer. After a moment of behaving like a distracted cow, I said, "I guess I'm prepared to roll with the punches. I mean, I know you have to do some minority hiring, 'life with the board' is so up in the air. I wouldn't mind staying here. I work well with the children. But if I can't stay, I'll work well with children somewhere else." I shrugged and smiled my best hippie-drifter girl smile.

"For a first-year teacher, well, you outshine teachers of three, four years!" (I love his qualifiers. Charming. He is right to be frugal with his compliments; he wouldn't want to run out, after all.) "But sometimes your attitude . . . it's like you don't want to play by the rules. It makes me peevish."

Flashback in my mind. Reading *Aesop's Fables* to the children. "And the fox said, 'I've heard you have the loveliest voice of all the birds in the forest! Dear Crow, how I long to hear you sing! If only you would release that cumbersome piece of cheese from your beak.'"

I laughed a girlish *ha-ha-ha*. "It seems to me that playing by the rules has not gotten the children of our city too terribly far. But that aside, I realize—and don't envy—the difficulty in your having to work with someone with such a stubborn adherence to principles." (In retrospect, I wonder if he confused "principle" with the homonym "principal." You know where I'd lay my bet.)

"You are stubborn," says he, "but in a lovable way. No matter what you do, I can't seem to stay angry."

"I envy that quality."

"I just wish you would understand. Rules made for one are for everyone . . ." blablablablaBLA. Whose rules? His rules? Michael Jordan's rules? God's rules? I thought, *I wanted to teach so I could lead, not follow.* I kept my trap shut.

"The bottom line is, I'm going to retain you. What do you think of that?"

"That's very nice," I lied. "I look forward to staying. I must be honest, though, that I am pursuing my instructional media endorsement and will leave in the event that a library accepts me." I have been secretly dreaming of becoming a school librarian, so I can have my favorite part of the day all day long: reading aloud.

"See, you're always *learning*, always moving *forward*. Makes you an *asset*, part of the *core* here. Now, there's going to be some *changes*, some *upheaval*, some teachers will have to go, but I don't want you to be nervous. You are going to be retained." He looked giddy and cheerful and got up. I extended my hand in a gesture of infinite generosity, which of course he overestimated and hugged me. Serious gross out! Then he left.

My pose upon his departure was that of pure maliciousness, as Snow White's stepmother looks into her mirror with squinting, plotting, viperous eyeballs. I have no intention of staying at this silly crap hole, with this silly man who tells us we don't need a metal detector, the kids are just bringing the guns in to *show*. So I am left to my own meager devices to screw him!

screw him! screw him! Yes, keep me here, long enough to collect health insurance, a decent first-year assessment, you dick! Keep me here to learn about Ms. Federman's Big Fight, to prove the cliché that what doesn't kill me will make me stronger!

Besides which, even if my retention were welcome news, how could I be happy when it is accompanied by the insinuation that a lot of teachers are in for a lot of heartbreak?

"Some change, some upheaval . . ."

PART III

"The race is not always
to the swift, nor the battle
to the strong—but that's
the way to bet."

—Damon Runyon

April 5

Yet another teacher's meeting. Mr. Turner has someone from the board giving us workshops, an educational chiropractor here to "align our curriculum."
He had us write our "unit titles" on big pieces of
newsprint, and then we hung them up in a row, so
everyone could see how everyone's teaching fits in
with everyone else's teaching. Basically, we were making lists of what our kids will know by the end of
the year, by topic. I thought my list was pretty basic,
with units including objectives like kids being able to
write letters, count and manage money, locate all the
states . . .

"You can't possibly teach all you say you can teach.

A teacher can teach a maximum of fourteen units per annum." It was water off this duck's back. I know what I can accomplish. Still, how annoying! One teacher cried when he told her her units didn't meet state guidelines. What a baby! I pointed out to the board of ed guy, "Can't we write up our paperwork so it looks like we're following state guidelines and do whatever we want?" I said, "Can't we just look at the scope and sequence they print in front of all the textbooks and use all the right verbage? What bureaucrat would be the wiser? Once we close the classroom door, who else but us knows what goes on?"

He conceded that technically, yes, I was correct, but that wasn't the right attitude to take. The crybaby looked more cheerful, though. It's like it never occurs to some people that they don't have to do what people tell them.

I call her a crybaby, but maybe after twenty years of teaching with the usual lack of appreciation from the board of ed, I'd cry, too. Maybe after the hundreth time of being told I'm Not Following Guidelines, I'd break down. She hangs beautiful bulletin boards in the hallway, spilling over the edges with children's artwork. Her baskets burgeon to bursting with tantalizing children's books, I know she bought them with her own money. She never raises her voice, but when she speaks, the children listen, hush each other. She keeps the love letters the children send to her, written in the penmanship she taught them to write, using the words she taught them to read. If I had a child, I'd want her for my child's teacher. Isn't that the real litmus test?

The closed-door teacher anarchy I suggested seems so scary in theory, but in reality, I see it already exists. In my opinion, the prefabricated curriculum and board mandates that are concocted to hide this state of affairs can work two ways. They can be benign suggestions that make talented inventors out of teachers. Or they can make it so people who don't have anything to share can still work, since their scripts are made up for them. Nobody really knows which is happening when the teacher closes the door. At worst, mediocrity. At best, miracles. This curriculum guy went to school, didn't he? He must know this is the case. Anyone who has ever had a really good teacher —or a really bad one—must know this. It isn't that the curriculum guy was *wrong*. Only, I wonder if he can see that the efforts to try to regulate teaching could limit learning as much as ensure it.

So much of teaching is sharing. Learning results in sharing, sharing results in change, change is learning. The only other job with so much sharing is parenting. That's probably why the two are so often confused. You can't test what sort of teacher someone will be, because testing what someone knows isn't the same as what someone is able to share. This will be different for every teacher.

I am operating from a position where I am personally vested in my approach, which any teacher will tell you is a privileged place to be. Does being personally vested make a teacher successful? Not necessarily. Does it make a teacher accountable? Absolutely.

Education's best-kept secret.

HOW TO TEACH LEARNING

Sing it
Seal it in an envelope
Twist it under a bottle cap
  "You Are a Winner!"

Tie it to the leg of a carrier pigeon
   and let it soar
Hoard it greedily, with your back turned
   Then share it with a magnanimous grin
     and glittering eyes
Make it a surprise,
   shining like a quarter
     under a pillow
Whisper it,
   like the tow of summer's breath
     through the willow
Or
Hide it
   just between the tart skin and sweet flesh
of an apple
Make it
Forbidden
Make it
Delicious
Then
   let the children
     bite

. . .

April 7

Good news! I won the coveted Dr. Peggy Williams Award for outstanding new teacher in the field of Reading and Language Arts, given by the Chicago Area Reading Association! They give me a few hundred bucks to spend on my classroom, too, *tra-la, tra-LA.* The very best part of all is that no matter what Mr. Turner tries to pull, he can't take that away from me. Another goodie to add to my *raison d'être,* my résumé. I'm quite surprised to have won, and very excited, too. I get to go to an awards dinner this Thursday. The head lady suggested I bring my principal. *Wah,* I could barely keep from laughing out loud. The other fun thing is that it will be announced at school tomorrow, and hopefully Mr. Curriculum Alignment will hear it. Put that in your board of education pipe and smoke it, pal!

Enough gloating. I'm glad to have won, but really, I'd rather not be a teacher. What I'd really love to be is an opera star, but I haven't got the voice for it—just ask my downstairs neighbor! Still, how I would love to

play the witch in Humperdinck's *Hänsel und Gretel*.
I'm studying the libretto.

> Halt!
> Hocus pocus hexenschuss
> Ruhr dich und dich deiss der fluss . . .

> Hurrop, hopp, hopp!

April 11

Rotten day at school. Why? I went in with a positive
attitude, but then a package of stickers was stolen and
that just made me so mad. It's so aggravating when
one of them decides to shit on me and the class like
that. It's just wrong, wrong, wrong. I tried to put it behind me, but it wouldn't go. I vowed at least to try not
to misdirect my frustration and be cheerful for the
kids who don't steal. But the children came back from
gym and clearly had not done their homework, so
they couldn't participate in the game show–style lesson I had planned. Greedy and slothful! I was disgusted, but I tried to maintain.

I failed. Got so mad, I told one kid I would rip his

tongue out and he'd have to bring in a parent if he wanted it back. See, already practicing for the witch's role!

It's depressing. I always start out well, smiling and whirling around like I'm on a commercial trying to sell them the rest of their lives with no down payment until July, but the kids act so fucking obnoxious, clucking their tongues, groaning, swearing. They are really such wimps, they can't do anything without a complaint. Also, they wouldn't know enough to step out of the way of a speeding train.

"You ask me to do my work too strict! Ask me nice."

"Will you do it if I ask you nicely?"

"No."

"Will you do it if I ask you in a tough way?"

"Yes."

"Then I'll have to ask you in a tough way, until you respond when I ask you nicely."

"Oh, okay."

GOD!

I HAVE TO listen to the line "putting it my way, but *nicely,*" from "Getting to Know You," sung by Gertrude

Lawrence in *The King and I* at least eight times before I walk out the door in the morning. In fact, I find myself living life more and more "to the tune of."

When I am feeling frustrated by Mr. Turner, I blast "Funkier than a Mosquita's Tweeter" by Tina Turner, "Nothing from Nothing" by Billy Preston, or perform an indignant solo tango to "Jealousy" by Jacob Gade from *Tango Argentino*.

When I am frightened, "Perpetuum Mobile" by Novacek and "Prelude and Allegro" by Kreisler, both performed by Itzhak Perlman.

When I need to love children more, "Tenderly" by Bill Evans, "The Beautiful Land" by Anthony Newley from *The Roar of the Greasepaint, the Smell of the Crowd,* or "Sing a Simple Song" by Sly and the Family Stone. "New York Charanga" by David Amram reminds me of girls skipping rope double Dutch and cheers me up.

When I fall short, it's time for "On How to Be Lovely" performed by Audrey Hepburn and Kay Thompson in *Funny Face,* "Control Yourself" performed by Jackie and Roy Kral, and "Every Day I Write the Book" by Elvis Costello.

Always, "Stoney End" by Laura Nyro.

Always, "Cabaret" performed by Jill Haworth.

Always, "Raindrops Keep Falling on My Head" by B. J. Thomas.

Always, "La Vie en Rose."

Always, lovely, spinning scratchy 33-rpm records, informing my teaching. I watch Billy pout and hear "Softly, William, Softly" by Dave Brubeck. I can hear Prokofiev's "Cinderella's Departure for the Ball" every time I have recess duty. Smetana's "The Moldau" is movement through the halls. Remembering these songs through the day overwhelms all of my senses. My imagination returns to the borderless fronts of my own childhood. The way the children run and leap, the fast and slow of adults intercepting them, it looks like a dance. I believe Mrs. Jones is about to *arabesque* as she passes out lunch tickets, or that Zykrecia is a dying swan in the throes of Kyle. The hairs on my arms and neck stand up. My back feels like ice. Then real sounds return to me, swelling, like the urgent, metallic ringing of an alarm clock rousing me from my dreams. It concerns me that I could be so engulfed in a fantasy that I am seeing and hearing things that others do not see or hear, however beautiful. At my age! I suppose an active imagination can be a form of madness. Or it can be the thing that keeps you from going mad.

April 15

I'm glad I didn't yell at Latoya today.

I almost yelled, "This is the fourth day in a row you're a half-hour late! You're missing important math instruction, and I don't appreciate repeating myself!" But then I remembered I promised myself to try not to single children out for public humiliation, which has been my *modus operandi* of late, but to talk—and listen—privately instead.

"Is there a reason you have been late four days in a row?" I asked her, alone in the hall.

"We are in a shelter this week, and I have to drop my little sister off and take the train over. It takes longer than I thought. I'm sorry, I'll be with my aunt next week and then I can walk over."

"Don't apologize. I'm proud of you for coming each day. It wouldn't be the same here without you, don't forget that. And even though we can't wait for you, if you miss an explanation in math, just ask me or a classmate . . ."

For the rest of the day I was glad I listened instead of yelled, but I still burned with shame at the thought of what I almost said and at all the occasions I have spoken harshly.

May 2

Akila gave me a sari, blue and pink and gold, really beautiful. I put it on immediately and wore it for the rest of the day. Grown-ups kept asking me, "What character are you today?"

When I called Akila's mom to thank her, she thanked me and said I helped Akila feel less self-conscious about her culture. She said that as we spoke, Akila was playing dress-up. She had put on sari number eleven.

"Pretending to be you," I said.

"I haven't been able to get her to wear a sari since we came to this country," said Akila's mother. "I think she's pretending to be *you*."

To further encourage Akila, I wore a *salwar kameez* I had. Monique, Asha, Latoya, and Akila all met me at the door this morning dressed in beautiful saris. Akila lent them out. Mr. Turner thinks we are having some sort of cultural festival. "Good. That's what democracy is all about," he says.

May 4

B. B. has been wild, threatening other kids and being rude to grown-ups. He even ran out of gym class. He came to my room, which surprised me. He just looked sad. We sat in the dark, eating chocolate chip cookies. I told him that I knew he loved his mother and that he could be a big help to her right now by making good behavioral choices so she wouldn't have to come to school. I told him I was angry because I knew he would grow up and forget me and not send me a free ticket when he works in an orchestra, playing the recorder. He smiled and giggled. He relaxed.

Still, he can't stop. He starts freaking out around 1:20. I can practically set my watch to it. Something clicks in him. It occurs to him that he doesn't want to go home or something. His dad is there in a wheelchair because he was critically shot in gang cross-fire.

So he gets in this big pounding fight on the playground at recess. When I broke them up, he called me a bitch. That was the last straw.

I had a private conference with Mr. Turner. "I'm sick of what kids get away with at this school. The kids are maniacs!"

"Don't let the parents hear you say that." Mr. Turner looked from left to right, ever the public relations vigilante.

"I don't come to work to be called a bitch or a cunt or a white whore," I informed him. "Isn't it part of your job to see that teachers aren't subjected to such behavior? Is it my job to spend all day disciplining so the children who want to learn can have a fighting chance?"

"You don't understand. They're black."

I blinked. "So, I shouldn't expect them to learn?"

"It's just the way black people are. The black child is different. They deal with so much. Drugs, gangs . . ."

"I grew up with black people. They didn't all act like this."

"That was a long time ago." He shook his head.

What, eight, ten years ago? "It's not about being black," I argued. "It's about being poor, and from people expecting nothing from you, and from nothing happening when you say 'Fuck you' to your teacher. Children rise to meet our expectations, good or bad." I felt myself talking a lot, mostly to block out what he was saying. I don't want to think the way he thinks. He can't be right. If he's right, it's not even worth trying. But I couldn't believe that he, a black man, was saying it. If I said that kind of trash, I'd expect to be strung up by my thumbs by members of my own ethnicity. I thought, *You wouldn't dare talk this way to me if I were black. You're telling me the ugliest part of you because you think because I'm white, I'll buy it. Fuck you,* I thought. *Fuck you!*

"We don't want to lose you. You're so young and creative. If you can't handle it, take a day off."

"It's not a question of whether I can do my job. It's a question of whether you can do yours." He looked at me, offended, but I didn't look away, because I felt real mad. "I believe there's a discipline code in this board of education, and I'll expect you to hold to its guidelines. Same as white suburban kids have rules, these black kids can have rules. If they can't, maybe the union can explain to me why not."

B. B. was suspended.

So why don't I feel like I won this one?

May 9

I've been really nervous about B. B. coming and shooting me. I don't know why I've been so nervous. I know the gang involvement is there, and there's so much about it that I can't understand, so I fear it. I repress it as best I can, but sometimes it surfaces. Will I be shot by a student? So many of them have guns at home. Why will I be shot? For suspending, scolding, letting someone cut in line, for giving too much homework? Ismene was right. School is different now, it's not like you can come in and teach that Columbus sailed in 1492 and 2 + 2 = 4. I also have horrific daymares of my students being shot or shooting themselves. The idea will flash across my mind, sometimes just during a quiet moment in class. I push it out of the front of my mind, but it quivers in the back with an eerie hum, like strings on a bow that has just shot a poison arrow.

I feel a certain ill ease about the human race and its unpredictable nature, its folly, its abuse of children. I look around and see that even grown-ups are really children, making mistakes and needing love. Does being wrong make you weaker? Does being needy make you weaker? I find myself praying, wishing for God, wishing for someone who sees everything that's happening, someone who cares what's happening. Maybe it's because it's so hard being the only grown-up in the room all day long.

Dear God. Make me a better person. Allow me the luxury of abhorring that which is bad. Help me to look shocked.

I never look shocked. Only annoyed.

The older teachers don't seem to have this problem. They seem to look annoyed only when talking about their ex-husbands or sex. They are so magnanimous with the children, like sows with a million teats. They talk about the children's home lives. They inquire. They want to know.

What is there to know? That they are beaten? That

their parents are illiterate, in jail, turning tricks, making them turn tricks? That they are hungry, filthy, that they watch their brothers and sisters late into the night? That they are living in the shelter? That the gangs are recruiting them, that they brought a gun to school?

All a bunch of gossip. But bend an eyebrow here and there, let out little breaths, then it is concern. Then it is love.

Dear God. Help me to love the little children.

May 10

Well, B. B. didn't shoot me, and he came in with his mom, Rowisha. She went into the details of his father's spiraling decline. Things are really hard at home. So if he starts acting out, she explained, it would be a big help if I didn't call.

I told her I felt sympathetic and wanted to help, but this is a school with lots of kids and lots of problems, and he is only welcome here insofar as he can be kind and safe. I told her that getting into a fistfight and calling me a bitch is neither kind nor safe.

At this point Rowisha turned around and started

pounding B. B. with both fists until he fell to the floor, right there in the hall. It reminded me of when Twanette was beaten in front of me. Why are the children who are beaten the ones I end up fearing the most?

B. B. shriveled and whined. She screamed about his behavior and gang involvement and how she's-not-even-going-to-think-about-it-I'll-just-have-your-ass-hauled-into-juvenile-next-time-you-do-any-such-bullshit. I pulled her off of B. B. She stormed off, disappearing around a corner. B. B. was hysterical, so I picked him up and hugged him and kissed him on the forehead and stroked the top of his head and told him it was going to be all right. Then Rowisha came back and hollered, "Don't *baby* this son of a bitch, his stupid ass doesn't deserve it," and punched him once more. I still tried to help him get it together. In ten minutes he was going to have the Iowa Standardized Test of Basic Skills administered to him.

May 11

Ozzie's grades are plummeting. When I called the mom in to talk about it, she started to bawl. She told me a lot of stuff I didn't know. Her old boyfriend was a drug fiend who set the transient hotel they were living in ablaze, burned it to the ground last Thanksgiving. Then she and Ozzie and Ozzie's four-year-old brother, Mohammed, were homeless for a couple of months. Then she got Ozzie a new stepfather, or whatever, who beats her up and calls Ozzie a pussy whenever he cries over it. He won't obey the restraining order. Ozzie put a gun to this stepfather's head, but she talked him out of shooting it. I was very surprised Ozzie did this. He isn't that way. He's gentle. He was pushed. Why do these dumb fucks keep guns around the house? They make the world as ruinous as they imagine it is. But that's another story, or another chapter of the same one. Ozzie's mom says Ozzie cries for me at night, wanting to talk to me, that he feels alone in the world. Everyone is so unhappy. I wonder if I can rise to the challenge.

May 12

Storyteller's Workshop is going well. I got a small grant. After school a couple of times a week, I train about a dozen children to give dramatic performances of folktales. I specifically picked children who are particularly shy or challenged in reading or speaking. We went on a field trip to see a professional storyteller, and they all own copies of the books they are going to perform. For the past six weeks I've been training them, modeling for them, and—to some extent—pressuring them. I had them go "on tour" to other classes during school hours to help them gain confidence and to get feedback. We are hosting a school-wide storytelling festival in less than two weeks.

Maurissa didn't want to perform for the fourth grade. Her dark skin paled to the color of ash, she was so afraid. I sent her with Ruben and Latoya, to watch and support her. She begged me not to make her go. Secretly, I wondered if she would throw up. But I literally pushed her out the door anyway and told her not to return until the mission was accomplished, that I knew she could do it. She came back fifteen minutes later—I should say leapt in—smiling broadly, her color back to normal.

"I did it! I did a beautiful job." She burst out laughing and crying at the same time, and we embraced.

Rochelle, another shy girl I sent out, returned breathing heavily. "You were right! The kids did join in on the repeated lines." I'm so proud of their successes. I know in the face of the wide world these are small victories, but sometimes a little song is sweet to hear, even if an orchestra is more accomplished.

May 13

The testing continues. I had to proctor for the Iowa Standardized Test of Basic Skills in the other fifth-grade room. I found them to be a surly bunch. Mrs. Jones still has up a winter scene and February's calendar. After two hours in her room, I felt depressed and bored. The children ignored simple directions and were vicious and insulting to each other. Many of them smiled at me, although they constantly defied me. I didn't see the need to lay down my iron fist; I knew I'd be leaving them shortly. Even though we have our share of problems, I breathed a sigh of relief to return to my own room with its colorful mess and cheering children, who clapped when I entered and all talked at once to tell me about their testing experience.

Mrs. Jones once cried in front of her class. A girl came running up to me in the hall after I had dismissed my class, saying, "Come comfort Mrs. Jones." I didn't know what she meant, but it sounded bad.

When I got there, Mrs. Jones was at her desk sobbing, mascara running Tammy Faye Baker–style, weeping, "I've lost my craft, I've lost my craft."

I dismissed her class and tried to comfort her because she felt so embarrassed. I told her it would be good for them to see that teachers have feelings, too. She cried because some kid gave her the finger.

May 16

Asha brought her two-year-old brother to school. No mama, no note, no nothing. I was concerned. It seemed illegal for the baby to be in my care with no parental permission. I tried to call Asha's apartment, but she admitted to giving a false number, that there was no phone. So I walked around teaching with a baby in one arm all day. That's a long day for a two-year-old. I kept expecting, though I knew it was naive, for the mom to show up, but she never did. Asha's father is still under in-house arrest. He came on parent night, though. He told me I had nice hair and that he'd beat Asha when he got home, she's due for it. He also asked me where Asha goes after school. He seemed very angry when I told him I really didn't know.

In retrospect, I should have told the administration that there was a baby in the building, but I was afraid they'd make Asha feel bad about it or do something weird—I don't know what, they overreact so. What else could they have done other than what I did?

I DON'T INTERFERE much. I shouldn't be so anthropological about it, but I am. I just let them live out the awfulness of childhood, like I lived it out, and try to advise them to make choices that they can live with later on. I'm so exhausted, run down, every day. My whole life is different. When someone asks me, "How was your day?," I never know what to answer. I have thirty-one days every day, a different day with each child. A good day with Ruben, a rough day with Billy . . . it's too much. They talk about rewards and gratification in teaching school, and there is a share of it, but they don't tell you it's like joining a monastery or going to hell or sleepwalking or being afraid, afraid as you were when you were small. They don't tell you how it feels when you get dizzy in front of a room full of children, or what it feels like to tug at the tense bodies of children lashing, hating, fighting, spitting, scratching. They don't tell how it feels to hear "I hate you!" or how it feels to say, "That's okay, I still love you." They say now, in the education classes, "You have to be everything to them: counselor, mother, friend . . ." on and on: The List. I hear the ones who have been teaching for many years run it off with a certain pride. Well, I don't think it's anything to be proud of. I don't want to play mama, I can't play mama. They need a real mama. And they need a real teacher.

May 21

Yesterday was the storytelling festival. I've been working like mad to prepare for it all week long. I was very nervous about the kids doing a lame job, even though I've been training them for six weeks. I was mostly nervous because people from the grant foundation were coming to observe. But the festival was, I thought, a great success.

The kids and I set up two performance areas in the library, one with mosquito netting and big foil stars hanging like a starry night, and the other covered with gold sari material and a big cardboard smiling sun. We set up a bake sale, and the bookstore where I used to work let me use books for a book sale. I finally got to use some of my ideas from my old Fairy Tale Festival proposal. I made a carnival game, "The Three Billy Goats Gruff Toss," with a little basketball net, that kids could play for free and win bookmarks or chocolates. The performances were after school. Kids could come of their own accord. Over a hundred showed up. As they entered, they were alternately given a paper butterfly or a paper smiley face. They enjoyed the peripheral attractions. I had divided the performers into two groups, so the performances would be suitable length for younger children's attention spans. I announced for the kids holding butterflies to go to the sun stage and kids holding smiley faces to go to the star stage.

That way, both sets of performers had a pretty equal audience.

By God's mercy, the children quieted down quickly. I had two MCs to introduce the performers. I didn't have to do anything. The performances were in full swing when the grant women arrived. I was free to greet them warmly and maneuvered them back and forth between the stages to watch the strongest performances. At the end, each of the performers got flowers and a certificate and much-deserved applause. The grant women were delighted. They told me to apply again next year, that they would remember my name. Meanwhile, there were children everywhere, involved in everything.

The grant women asked me if my administration was supportive. Before I could answer diplomatically, in walked Ms. Coil and Mr. Turner, after the fact. Mr. Turner was visibly appalled at the liveliness and began pleading noisily for the gratuitous silence that he so adores. He said, first thing, "Don't you think we should have had this in the Commons Area instead of the library?"

"No," I answered flatly. Mr. Turner and Ms. Coil stared over the scene, unimpressed, until the grant women were introduced and they started *ooohing* and *ahhing*. Then Ms. Coil said, "Can't you do it over so we can videotape it and send it to the Jordan Foundation?" This made me extra mad, because I had asked them to videotape it earlier, and they didn't. It also proved they didn't understand or appreciate what had occurred; over one hundred kids had been sitting quietly watching ten at-risk kids perform, and perform well, without any prompting whatsoever. The stages had been taken down, the bake sale and book sale were being cleaned up, didn't they see?

"It was a happening," I shrugged, "but it's already happened."

I really hate them.

The other teachers were supportive. Mrs. Rae was the best, helpful and encouraging. She said, "This was amazing!" I kept thinking of her saying that, and the way she lent a hand without my even asking. Her support felt so good, like a little warm glowing coal inside of me.

While I was talking to the grant women, a third

grader came up to me and said, "I want to be a story-teller, and I want to see more stories. Can we do this again tomorrow?" It was so gratifying. I don't know if everyone enjoyed it, but I know it was nice for a few kids, and Ismene used to tell me that if you can do that in a real way, that's the most you can ever hope for as a teacher.

I don't mean to show off, but I can't tell anyone else the compliments I got or it would seem too stuck up. Still, I want to write them because I really do feel proud of myself. I feel good, like I did something I wanted to do and it turned out like I imagined, and in life that doesn't happen too often.

May 22

Hauled my ass out of bed to teach today. I'm having to teach sex ed, which is more uncomfortable than I thought it would be. The board mandates "Family Life Education," and insists that we show this video that's really old and corny-feeling, like a filmstrip. Mrs. Jones wanted both of our fifth-grade rooms to watch it together, since she was really nervous and wanted moral support. So we watched in her room. It showed a cartoon of a goldfish pooping out eggs and another fish pissing out sperm. "A fish has eggs," the video droned, "and a dog has eggs. A sheep has eggs. A giraffe has eggs. And a woman has eggs." I'm not usually compared to a dog, sheep, and giraffe in such a brief span of time. My girls looked perplexed, too, as though they were destined to someday poop out eggs for their boyfriends to piss on. Indeed, as we filed out of the room, JoEllen whispered urgently, "Madame, am I going to lay an egg?"

Back in our own room, I did my best to eradicate the damage the video had done and fielded other questions. They asked about birth control, abortion, homosexuality, all the stuff I was told at in-services not to teach about. I still answered them but prefaced everything with "Well, from my point of view . . ." and ended with ". . . But be sure to talk about it with your family, because everyone's values are different."

"What if I don't agree with my family?" asked Ruben.

"Then try to wait until you grow up to express it."

It's hard for me to teach this because I won't say homosexuality is wrong or unnatural, and I won't say wait until marriage to have sex. The only thing I didn't really answer is how an abortion works, because I thought it was too creepy and unnecessary for fifth graders to know about. I have to keep reminding myself to stay scientific and not to talk about how to have a cheerful sex life when you grow up. I know I'm teaching it all wrong, I'm too pleasant about it, even though I feel very tense and wonder if a parent is going to respond. I don't even want to write about it anymore. It's just another example of how I'm supposed to teach what they should get at home: teacher as unwilling extended family.

May 23

Like clockwork, B. B. was being a dick after lunch, hurling obscenities at everyone. I moved him off a bit while I read *King Matt,* but he was still being a dick, mumbling and talking. I gave a second warning. He kept jabbering rude things under his breath, like those crazy people on the bus. I felt as exasperated as I've been all year.

"Would you please stop acting like a jerk?"

"Fuck you! I'm not a jerk! You're a jerk!"

Immediately, I knew I had made a mistake. No similes are allowed in kid-speak.

"Did I call you a jerk?"

"Yes!"

"No, she didn't," Selena called out. "She said you're *acting* like a jerk, which you *are*."

"Regardless, I apologize. I shouldn't have said that," I offered.

B. B. continued his stupid mumbling.

I caught him in the hall on his way to his mandatory after-school tutoring program. I told him I was really tired of him taking out his anger on me and the class, that it hurt me and made me feel worried about him, and that he'd better tell me what was going on if he didn't want to get suspended again. I plopped down on the stairs and told him to do the same.

"Want to talk about your dad being shot?"

Silence.

"How do you feel? Happy? Sad? Like you want to get those guys? What?"

"I don't want to talk about it."

"Do you want to talk about your dad before he got shot? Was he nice? Cruel? What?"

Silence.

"Want to talk about your little sister and the fact that you're the one taking care of her?"

"No."

"Want to talk about your mom?"

"No."

"Want to talk about school? Your friends? Me? How much you hate me for asking?"

"I don't have to answer any of your dumb questions." He smiled, his eyes narrowing.

"You're absolutely right. I don't even have any right to ask them. Kind of like you don't have any right to act so abusive toward me and the class. You think you're not telling me about your problems, but you're showing me, every day and in every way. The problems aren't going to leave until you start talking about them."

He got up, burst out crying, and started stomping away.

"You'll have to walk a lot faster than that to leave your problems behind," I called after him, but I didn't follow him.

I sat on the stairs and got more and more aggravated, thinking about recent things that have happened concerning B. B., like how his mom asked me for money so he could go to the carnival. How his mom told me B. B. said, "Mama, you don't love me because you keep trying to send me away." How I arranged for a mentor to come spend time with B. B., a professional, upstanding black man, to counter his father's influence, and he didn't show up. He didn't come through. Everyone—just not coming through for B. B.

I had him called out of tutoring to the counselor's office. "It's crisis proportion, for me and for him," I explained, in front of him. "B. B., you're so angry, it makes me feel unsafe, it interrupts the learning of your classmates." I turned to the counselor. "I've documented unsuccessful interventions since November. What are you going to do?"

She sent B. B. out of the room and said, "I don't know."

In the end she called him back in and said she was going to send a note home. He started bawling.

"Why are you crying like that? Your mom will beat you when she sees that note, won't she?" I asked.

"I'll make a deal," said the counselor. "I won't send the note home tonight. But if you act up tomorrow, I hand-deliver it to your house. Is that a deal? What do you think, Madame Esmé?"

Frankly, I don't like making deals with kids. "I don't know . . . What do you think, B. B.?" He was pouting. The tears hadn't gotten him where he had expected. "Whoops! Can't make a deal with a rock. If you can't look at me and talk like a person, no deal. Sorry."

He started bawling again. The counselor escorted him down the stairs to leave. He collapsed into an hysterical heap on the way down, weeping uncontrollably, and told how he is beaten at home.

It's not news. I'm not surprised. The counselor isn't going to really do anything except feel sorry for him, and there's not much I can do aside from call the Department of Children and Family Services and make it all turn into a bigger nightmare.

It's just that I wanted him to say it, name it, so he can see it, taste it, know the enemy of his sorrow, and learn that he can be bigger than it, not let it rule him. Too tired to write more. I've stopped making sense.

. . .

June 2

Melanie is so busted!

She was already in trouble for stealing Ms. Coil's checkbook with Vanessa. They managed to get sixty dollars out. Now they are on juvenile probation and were supposed to help the janitor every day after school for the rest of the year, cleaning toilets and stuff. Melanie confided in her journal that she kind of liked doing it, it felt like she had a job. But then she was cleaning in a teacher's room, and the janitor was called away. She went into the teacher's desk and found some change. She had her hands in the desk when a teacher from another class walked in. "What are you doing?" she asked.

"Ummm, looking for a puppet play script?"

The teacher told me when she gave such a creative answer, she knew she must be from my room, so she came to tell me Melanie was in the office.

When I went down, Melanie was sitting alone in Ms. Coil's office. Melanie burst out crying and trembling and threw her arms around my shoulders. I held her and whispered, "Melanie, I know I told you practice makes perfect, but I really don't think you're ever going to be a good thief."

She broke into laughter.

I continued, in my most doctorlike voice, "Now, where did you start to feel it?"

"Feel what?"

"The feeling. You know, Melanie. Didn't you get a weird tickly feeling when it occured to you to take something that wasn't yours?"

She looked shocked. "Yes."

"Well, where did it start? In your toes? On the back of your neck? In your knees?"

"No," she said, very definitely, "it was in my stomach. My stomach." She burst into tears again.

"Did you feel it there the time you were about to steal Ms. Coil's checks?"

She was bawling so hard she couldn't speak, but she nodded.

"Why are you crying, then?" I asked. "That's wonderful. You're very lucky. You know the signal of when you're about to steal. So you can stop it. Whenever you get that feeling, you can run and find me and say, 'Madame, my stomach hurts in that special way,' and

I'll give you something else to do. Just one more thing, though, Melanie. Did you get that feeling when you took my stickers?"

"Yes," she squeaked and threw herself into my arms, crying. "I'm sorry, I'm sorry . . ."

I pulled her away and looked into her face. "This is very bad, all this stealing. If you get caught again, I won't help you. Ms. Coil will want to send you to the audi-home, and I won't help you. Believe me when I say I love you, but believe me just as much when I say I'll let you go to the live-in reform school, the *audi-home,* if you pull this again! *Audi-home,* where you'll meet some girls who will teach you the meaning of the word *sorry*! I know you are smart and can stop it if you try, so if you do it again, it's just because you disrespected me by not listening, so I won't help. Do you understand?"

Ms. Coil came in with a policeman and Melanie's mother. Melanie clenched my hand like a woman in labor when she saw the cop, but I freed it. "We had a good talk," I said. "A lot is worked out."

Melanie's journal entry after returning from three days' suspension:

"I shamed oh god my life. Madam was right it in my stummuck but then I git home it all over my body, this bad filling. It so boring at home I fill sick bad. Now I back and everybody think I bad. Why Vanessa tell me to do that oh no oh no, and the worse part when momma come in the offis Madam look at me like Im not even there"

No, you know what I think the worse part is? I think Melanie's going to have to repeat the fifth grade.

June 4

Little thoughts:

Billy hasn't given me any real problems since he taught.

Kyle performs better in math if I let him stand on his head whenever he wants.

Ashworth could be a children's author and illustrator someday, his drawings are so bold, his writing so direct.

Ruben draws muscle men in his journal but hides from the gangs after school in the public library.

Selena is shrewd, a poor sport, and walks with an

affected palsy in her wrists and a hunch in her shoulder. She is a little old lady in disguise.

Samantha is a genius, strange and alone, a girl lost in a forest with nothing but a pen, searching for a friend to write to. I helped her start a sticker collection. It's her big hobby now. I want her for my little sister.

Asha complains noisily at the start of read-aloud time, and at the end, too. She has serious eyes, sensitive. She deserves love.

Letter from Maurissa: "I really think that you are helpful when it comes to dressing up."

June 8

Ozzie has been complaining of stomachache after lunch almost every day for the past week and a half. I thought he might just be tired, or maybe a little food poisoning, but the other children don't complain. Today we were walking to gym and he started to vomit. I held his head over the toilet in the teachers' bathroom. The rest of the class stood in the hall and waited. Nobody said anything and nobody acted up. I was glad.

June 9

The counselor showed me the kids' Iowa reading and math scores. Best in the school, she said. At least one-year jump for almost everyone, and several kids jumped two and three years.

I feel like we did a lot of interesting things this year. Some of my favorites: When learning about electricity, we made light-up quiz games. When learning about light, we put on shadow-puppet shows. When learning medieval history, we built an accurate castle, then decorated it with colored marshmallows and put it in our fairy tale book display. When we learned about air, we had a bubble festival. When learning about Asia, we made sushi. We made video commercials to promote our favorite books. We had a book character masquerade party. We went to an outdoor Beethoven concert and visited Buckingham Fountain downtown. The kids had checking accounts in a classroom economy. We had a cereal box supermarket, and the kids learned to make change. We had formal debates on T.T.W.E. topics. We made a book of fables. My kids write the best descriptive compositions. They have international pen pals. They illustrated poetry anthologies. They read and wrote treasure maps. They know all the dances from the 1960s.

Ismene said, "When you have a classroom of your own, you just can't *do* every idea that you think of." I feel I came pretty close. I am fried as an egg. My personal relationships have suffered. I see now why so many of the older teachers are divorced. I am tired and lonely, but the children have enjoyed a measure of success. It can go on their permanent records. For what it's worth.

June 10

Today I went into the lunchroom early to pick them up, to see if I could find out why Ozzie gets sick. Sure enough, his lunch tray was piled up with hamburgers, in a horrible mound, and he was eating them. *All* of them!

"Jesus Christ, Ozzie. You can't eat like this. That's why you're getting sick, don't you see?" I took the tray away and found the lunch monitor, another first-year teacher. "Does he eat like this every day?"

"The kids give him whatever they don't want, and he eats it," she shrugged.

"And you let him?" I felt my voice rising. "Look, you can't let him. He's overweight for one thing, and for another, it makes him puke. There's eleven fucking burgers here. It makes *me* want to puke. Two of anything. That's the limit. Okay?"

Useless idiot! Stands there watching a kid eat himself sick.

I explained to Ozzie that two is the limit, and I explained to the rest of the class that they've got to help. He looked nervous. I took him aside and told him it would be all right, that he didn't have to worry about being hungry like he was last year when he was homeless.

June 15

I can't believe it. Yesterday, he called me into his office about "Madame" again. AGAIN! WHY? WHY? WHY? WHY? WHY? WHY? WHY?

Two questions:

1) Why does he care?

2) Why do I care?

Doesn't Shakespeare say, "That which we call a rose/By any other name would smell as sweet"? Yes, it's true. But someone who goes around calling a rose another name—a daisy, an elephant, a peanut butter sandwich—is either a poet or an idiot, and Mr. Turner is no poet. I've had the poor fortune of learning my own name, knowing it deep inside, and it isn't Miss, Mrs. or Ms. It's Madame, *Madame,* MADAME! It just is! That's why it's so likely that I argue about it with him. To call me something else seems so absurd, it is as if when he says "You are not madame," he is really saying the equivalent of "You are a peanut butter sandwich," which is why I have to snicker when he keeps insisting over and over. He gets madder and madder, like a little boy having a tantrum, demanding that everyone call every animal a "doggie" even when it is not a dog. That's all fine, but it is so hard for me to humor him to the extent that he clamors to be humored.

After our latest battle, I walked outside, and a Jamaican lady came up to me from out of nowhere and told me Jah loves me, Jah has blessed me, that she could see I was an intelligent girl who could see and valued the uniqueness of each one in the world. It was odd. She embraced me, even though I didn't know her. I thanked her anyway and told her she came at a time when I needed her. Then I felt renewed and calm and felt the desire to stop asking why I am the way I am, why I'm so weird. Those questions are for other people to ask about me.

But then I continued to waste my energy, writing Mr. Turner a hateful note and talking to the union rep. I thought, I really like parts of my job, and I don't want to lose it, but why do I have to pretend that up is down and black is white and Mr. Turner is right in order to keep it?

I've been up in the middle of the night, wondering, *Why do I care? Am I crazy?* A little, maybe.

Then, after school today, Samantha's second-grade brother, Marky, walked into my classroom. The boy walked in so quietly. He said hello to me and then proceeded to the audio center. He listened to a book tape, gently turning pages for twenty minutes. Then he said, "I'll be back tomorrow." He's a boy with severe behavioral disorders. Usually he runs to hug me in the morning. One morning he was feeling so much hostility that he ran up to me and punched me in the jaw and burst out crying. I automatically put him into a body lock, like I learned in Classroom Management in college, and lowered him into a seated position until he calmed down. I couldn't believe I was actually doing it, like a reflex. My jaw didn't hurt, but I was surprised at how volatile he was. I wasn't angry. I know it sounds crazy, but I think he socked me because he loves me and felt he could be free to react with me.

But in my classroom, he sat so quietly . . . He looked so happy . . .

Ms. Federman is right. I can't win.

But I can play.

Just call me a peanut butter sandwich in a black-is-white world.

June 28

Last day of school. Had the kids write letters to the next class of fifth graders. It was neat to see what the kids remembered most. I like Asha's letter:

The things you will learn are fractions, the preamble, the Bill of Rights, Beethoven, and explorers, enventers, learn about planets like Saturn. You also will learn about solar power. You might read *King Matt*, *Tikki Tikki Tembo*, *The Wish Giver*, *Number the Stars*, *The Empty Pot*, *The Hundred Dresses*, *What's So Funny Ketu*, *Herschel and the Hanukkah Goblins*, *The Sneetches*, *The Bat-Poet* and *The Big Orange Splot.*

The rules are no saying shut up or bad language.

You should be good in Madame Esmé's class cause she can be real mean.

Zykrecia wrote:

In my class our rules are never say shut up to anyone, don't talk back to the teacher but we sometimes do it anyway and no chewing gum but we do that anyway. My advice is to try hard on your work and be real nice and listen and cooperate with your teacher and classmates . . . and just because someone's messing with you you don't have to beat them up unless you want to.

Zowela:

If you guys are worried if she's mean don't
be because she is one of the most nicest
teacher I ever had. If your nice to her she
will be nice to you. I am giving you my
word that you will have a wonderful time in
fifth grade. The teacher gives you jobs.
Every week she changes your job. Let me
tell you that my favorites are messenger,
postal worker, lunch ticket passer, line
captain, jokester. She read us this book
that has about 300 pages called *King Matt*,
maybe she will read it to you someday. One
more thing that I know you will love is
the Happy Box. If you answer a question
that she thinks is hard you get it. It's
filled with toys, stickers, bookmarks. Believe me, you will love this room.

Esther could barely write, she was crying nonstop
and saying God bless me.

In the back of the room, Rochelle's mom, a really
helpful parent, was working on a surprise for me.
It was a gold scarf with all the children's signatures
under the inscription:

Mme. Esmé;
> You taught us:
>> math, spelling, to enjoy reading, science, art, music. To enhance our written words, to speak with good diction.
>
> You taught us:
>> to be kind to our brothers and sisters (mankind), how to hold our heads up high. To not just try but try our best.
>
> You must wonder and ask, "Did I do O.K.?"
>
> The answer is NO!!!—You did Great!

Of course, I cried. There was so much I wanted to say. But the sands of the hourglass fell, and they left me, single file.

EPILOGUE

You have the right to work, but
for the work's sake only.
You have no rights to the fruits
of work. Desire for the fruits
of work must never be your motive
in working. Never give way to
laziness, either . . . Work done with
anxiety about results is far
inferior to work done without
such anxiety, in the calm of
self-surrender. . . . They who work
selfishly for results are miserable.

—from the Bhagavad Gita

Three years later, I am most surprised by how little has changed. When I hear the teachers at my new school talk about the graduating class, they say, "They've turned into real ladies and gentlemen! They're grown up!" But when I saw mine graduate today, my former fifth graders from the old school, they looked so much the same; perhaps their faces were a little less doughy, more defined. Are they stunted? Am I seeing them the way I will always see them? Am I the keeper of the ghosts of their childhood selves?

Mr. Turner was onstage with a background of rich blue velour drapes, giving motivational "directives" with his clearly enunciating, almost robotic delivery.

Beside me, the discontented murmurings of Ozzie's mother, who couldn't get hold of a camera. All around me, the alarming majority of parents chewing gum like there is no tomorrow. Some mothers sport hairdos as tall and elaborate as ice sculptures. Onstage, some honor students, girls wearing new white high-heeled shoes (unscuffed), stockings (unrun). The back of children's heads, caps and gowns, sitting straight, behaving. Little exhausting efforts to make this day elegant. I myself changed my outfit before coming. No silver shoes. No miniskirt. No shock. A flowered dress, a small nose ring. I am getting old.

Also exhausting: speeches about paying the price, success, follow your dreams, achievements of the past, achievements of the future. What about the present? The speeches begin to sound like pleas. "There's nothing for you on the streets," a teacher's voice is amplified. The gum-chewing parents applaud. Do they say this at white-kid graduations? Do they dress up like this everywhere when children graduate eighth grade? Look at the floral arrangements some parents have brought. Look at the cops outside—in case. This is a big deal. Someone crossing the stage is celebrating their only graduation. Should we hold our applause or let it thunder forth?

ISMENE ONCE TOLD me, "The difference between a beginning teacher and an experienced one is that the beginning teacher asks, 'How am I doing?' and the experienced teacher asks, 'How are the children doing?' " Sitting in the audience, I wonder where the other sixteen of my thirty-one fifth graders are today. They aren't crossing the stage to graduate. Did they move? Did they fail? Then I begin to regress. Where am *I* today?

I stayed at Mr. Turner's school for two years. The second year, he gave me a lesser rating because I used up half of my sick days. "If you loved teaching, you wouldn't have gotten pregnant," he explained.

And yet today, I don't feel my usual hatred toward Mr. Turner. He is far away from me, onstage, impotent. He is cursed: a man with a platform, an audience, and nothing of his own to say.

Besides, I should be happier now. My new principal is a true professional and has more faith in me than I have in myself. She held a school librarian position for me while I raised my son through his first year. She didn't shame me for wanting to be a mother. "Family first," she said. "Here we want you to have a life outside of these walls. We'll wait. I know you'll be worth waiting for."

As if that initial kindness wasn't enough, after a year of thank you notes in my mailbox, she called me into her office and gave me a superior rating. She seemed shocked when I started to cry. She apologized. I opened my mouth to explain, but couldn't decide what to say.

. . . but I didn't break up any fights!

. . . but I didn't take any children home to hide!

. . . but I didn't do an assembly program!

. . . but I didn't bring in an author!

. . . but I didn't raise standardized test scores!

. . . but I didn't fear for my life!

. . . but . . . they don't ask for my love here!

Instead, I just buried my face in my hands and choked. "I tried so hard there. It was never enough. I don't work here like I worked there. I worked my ass off, and he never once . . ."

"You can't really think that you don't do anything here, do you?"

So, my principal now is Glinda to my Dorothy. So why aren't I happy? Is it the teachers here, drunk on worksheets and gossip? Is it the students, clean and coddled, polite excuse-makers? Is it the mothers with their lemonade smiles, employed husbands, and tantrums when their children get C's? I've heard that a posse of them rail on me weekly at the local manicurist. "She works them so hard! That librarian, who does she think she is!" Some come in person, and as they yell and gesture, I can't help but imagine them speaking a subconscious monologue: "How dare you! Don't you know my child is white? Don't you know he has mastery of conventional grammar? Don't you know we can afford college?"

Why am I not happy? I left an abusive job for a dispassionate one.

THESE THOUGHTS ARE dispelled, to my relief, by the lilting voices of two girls onstage now, singing so beautifully that I squint to make sure they aren't lip-synching. Wearing silver blouses and moving their hands through the air slowly, they are so much like mermaids. I cry for the first and only time during the ceremony, being reminded of what I am missing, yet being hard-pressed to define it.

People snicker, "Those who can't do, teach." But, oh, how right they are. I could never, ever do all I dream of doing. I could never, ever be an opera star, a baseball umpire, an earth scientist, an astronaut, a great lover, a great liar, a trapeze artist, a dancer, a baker, a buddha, or a thousand other aspirations I have had, while having only been given one thin ticket in this lottery of life! In the recessional, as I watch them, *mine*, the ones I loved, I overflow with the joyous greed of a rich man counting coins. Wrongly I have thought teaching has lessened me at times, but now I experience a teacher's great euphoria, the knowledge like a drug that will keep me: Thirty-one children. Thirty-one chances. Thirty-one futures, our futures. It's an almost psychotic feeling, believing that part of their lives belongs to me. Everything they become, I also become. And everything about me, they helped to create.

AFTERWORD

As I write this, the governor of a certain western state is proclaiming in an address that his state has too many inadequate teachers and students, but fear not, he declares, in *his* administration they will be held accountable. His state boasts the largest number of students and teachers in the U.S. and ranks last in reading scores. It also ranks last in school and public library support, two things he neglects to note in his speech. Perhaps he thinks more threats will be more effective than more books.

His speech comes on the heels of a dinner conversation I had with my neighbor, a first-year principal in a Northeast school district where her rural/suburban community students scored remarkably high on the state's new student proficiency test. So three weeks ago the chairman of the State Board of Education "honored" them with an inspection visit.

According to my neighbor, the chairman arrived in a limousine and largely ignored the warm welcome from students and teachers. He strode through the middle and elementary classrooms for two hours like Napoleon himself, avoided eye contact with one and all, pronounced ringing fault with student spelling and penmanship, and won the following citation from the metropolitan newspaper photographer assigned to the visit: "That was the rudest public performance I have seen in all my years at this job!"

It is people like these—the governor, the chairman of the state school board—whose press conferences too often set the tone for the public debate on education. One must wonder: Has either one of these people ever taught a class? If so, how long ago? Was it university level, high school, junior high, elementary, rural, inner-city, or affluent suburban? How often have they visited a modern classroom, arriving sans entourage or limousine and sitting as an observer of real live teaching and learning?

One must also wonder what they would think of

this book, *Educating Esmé*—if they could find the time to read it. Surely they would be shocked, as would most critics of the modern classroom. For one thing, Madame Esmé's bullet-holed classroom is so unlike the one in which "they" were taught. The buildings have changed, the students have changed, the parents have changed, the administrators have changed, but, nonetheless, the teachers and test scores aren't supposed to change.

I wonder how the all-knowing governor and chairman would have handled Esmé's challenges:

- when Twanette's mother confided that she was six months behind in the belt whippings of her naughty child but resolved to get ahead of schedule that night;
- when Esmé must purchase her own classroom library if students are to have anything but textbooks yet is faced with how to prevent theft by children who don't own a single book;
- when her field-trip bus is stoned by a neighborhood gang as the principal looks on passively from his office window;

- when she is told that black children cannot be taught like white children;
- when the morning's national anthem needs more than the monotonously unfeeling treatment it's been given for four consecutive classroom years;
- when the vice principal suggests Esmé help her move household furniture after school;
- when a fifth-grader brings her two-year-old brother to school for the day because there's no one at home except an abusive father who's under house-arrest.

Granted, the governor and the chairman might have been able to solve some of those problems— even as twenty-four-year-olds, but could they have solved them with the ingenuity, the panache, the élan of Esmé? Would either of them have invented a "time machine" for their classroom? Would they have confronted the obscenely macho principal or knuckled-under out of self-preservation?

Educating Esmé is not for the naive, the faint of heart, or the born-again idealist. It is not a how-to-teach book. Rather, it's a painfully candid, often inspiring personal accounting by a first-year teacher of thirty-one Chicago fifth-graders. And because it's a personal diary, the emotional content has not been prettied up for publication. The author lets all the linen hang out, the clean with the dirty. In her classroom, she confesses to moving within minutes from being a loving den mother to a child-devouring dragon. Yet even as a dragon, Esmé devours uniquely. She consumes her pupils with wit, threats, music, poetry, pouts, compliments, and—always, daily—literature.

Even more refreshing in a book about education, the author is not some professorial pedagogue steeped in the wisdom sifted from forty years in academia. She is young, rash, exuberant, alternately innocent and street-wise, always child-wise, and sometimes irrational. But she is *never* irrelevant.

Educating Esmé is terribly relevant to where we are in American education, behind the desk and in front of the desk, in the home and in the office.

Some would have us believe that only a return to the "good old days" of rote learning can produce the test results needed in today's society. So for all her brazenness with the curriculum, what, in the end, were the results when Esmé's troop of thirty-one renegades took the Iowa Standardized Test of Basic Skills? How effective were her electronic quiz games, the marshmallow castle, the bubbles festival, and the sushi menu? That's for you, the reader, to think about, and, please God, all the governors and school board chairs, too.

—Jim Trelease

Acknowledgments

I would like to thank the following people, who have been so instrumental in my teaching and writing: Jim Pollock; my parents, Barry and Betty Codell and Florence and André Pollock; my grandparents, Isidore, Rosalie, Evelyn, and Seymour; Robin Robinson; Ron Saiet; Rochelle Cueto; Elyse Martin; Heather Cella; Patti Taylor; Reggie Codell; Carrie Codell; Constance A. Roberts; David Newman; Andy Laties; Tom Caplan; Reverend Sheila Goggin; Sarah Packer; Betty Sitbon; Lana Nieves; Carol Aubot of the Aldrich Public Library in Barre, Vermont; Ann Miller; Cyril Ritchard; Conrack; Garrison Keillor; Jim Trelease; Caroline Feller Bauer; and my insightful and encouraging editor, Amy Gash. A special thanks to all the hard-working Chicago Public School teachers and aides and the children who make my days so interesting. A debt of gratitude to the memories of Constance Schultz, my angel, and Ismene Siteles, a teacher's teacher.

EDUCATING ESMÉ

HIT THE GROUND RUNNING

Designers of Possibility

Advice for Aspiring and
New Elementary School Teachers

New Teacher Shopping List

Designers of Possibility

At the risk of sounding like a teacher, I have to say it: the end of a book is not always the end of a story. For several years that followed the one described in *Educating Esmé,* I stayed on with the Chicago Public Schools. I came to love my job as a school librarian. In this role as another kind of educator, I savored meeting with all of the children in the school, reading aloud every day and, most of all, sharing so much information, so many beautiful visions of the way the world can be, so many reasons to laugh and cry and think and believe and build. Authors and illustrators forge otherwise impossible connections across time and space and between people, and the creators of such books are symbiotically joined with teachers as designers of possibility. I came to recognize that children's literature is our country's best hope for equalizing education, because a great book in the hands of a rich child is the same great book in the hands of a poor child. I also recognized that being the catalyst for this connection between children and artists was a very sacred trust and that it was what I wanted to do for a living. More than that, it was what I wanted to do for a life.

I was also fortunate enough to eventually work for and with many diligent and humane administrators—people who filled their positions instead of letting their positions fill them. This underscored for me how important it is for teachers to make changes and take initiatives that support their own survival within school systems. I am so glad I didn't believe people who said things were the same everywhere or that my expectations weren't realistic. Things are the way we make them to be.

And so, how are we going to make them to be? Some teachers treat their classrooms like science labs, some treat them like business offices, and others as art studios in which they join the children in painting a picture of a perfect year. I like to imagine what classrooms and curricula might look like in the future and what skills and knowledge elementary school children are going to need: subjects like environmental science, global studies, computer science, and media literacy; and with the resurgence of the "DIY" ("do-it-yourself") crafts movement and the need for America to manufacture again, utilitarian classes like home economics, shop, and even the fine and applied arts may yet make a comeback in urban schools.

After *Educating Esmé* came out, I resigned my school position in order to work on other projects and realize other dreams, including national advocacy for literature-based learning and read-aloud. I homeschooled my son through a crucial year, taught full time in a private, progressive setting, wrote several novels for preteen readers, and started the PlanetEsmé Bookroom, an independent venture in

Chicago, in which I opened a storefront resource collection of about twelve thousand children's books and offered free programming to my community.

Some of the most personally rewarding work I have done has been with new teachers and teachers-in-training. They still walk that line between the nuts and bolts of teaching and the dream; they are still negotiating between what they personally have to offer and what is required of them. In one exercise, I asked teachers-to-be to visualize and draw the environment that most reflected what they had to share. After some egging-on—and permission to really fantasize—they described classrooms with desk arrangements around koi ponds. With toadstools instead of desks. With basketball nets. Or sometimes, the thought of a sink, a new bulletin board, some patched drywall, or a working bulb for an overhead projector was enough to inspire a reverie. It's funny how so little can go so far in a classroom. Teachers have always made the best and most out of what they're given. Never mind making a silk purse out of a sow's ear; give a good teacher a sow's ear, and she can make a Fendi bag. So imagine what a teacher can do with something better than a sow's ear?

This courage to dream about the classroom and their role in the lives of children is what I hope both new and veteran teachers have taken from reading my diary. Whatever battles we choose, whether the classroom is indeed an office or lab or art studio or zoo or enchanted forest or basketball court, we are always designers of possibility. Whether we are old-fashioned or newfangled, I hope teachers can think big enough and manifest their visions in ways that encourage children to believe in the American Dream; and by that I don't mean a house, a dog, and two-and-a-half children; I mean the reward of bringing what you imagine to fruition, the promise that we are telling the truth to children when we say, "If you can dream it, you can do it." And to them, it will be utterly realistic, because we will have done it first.

Advice for Aspiring and
New Elementary School Teachers

- -

I am often asked for helpful hints and survival tactics for the first year of teaching, the choicest of which I have compiled here. The biggest mistake new teachers make is underestimating their own role in preparation. Even excellent and thorough teacher training can never cover all the bases; there has to be some independent effort in order to hit the ground running. Most of this effort involves collecting information and materials, envisioning, and planning. The further in advance you begin, the better.

1. Be congenial to the custodian and to the school secretary. That's actually an age-old "word to the wise." Office clerks and custodial engineers have unique insights and wield a lot of power in the building. Operations can screech to a halt when these folks aren't happy. Be as concerned about making a professional impression on support staff as you would be about impressing administrators.

2. Think about why you are a teacher in terms of what you have to share. If you teach because you "love children," well, that doesn't always get you through the days when the children's behavior seems a little less than lovable. If you are motivated instead by what you can *impart,* that can really shift your teaching into overdrive. Maybe you enjoy traveling or cooking or dancing or playing the guitar or solving mysteries. Maybe you are an enthusiast of poetry or history or sports or architecture; whatever it is, integrate it into your classroom environment and your curriculum. That seems really basic, but it's so easy to get caught up in mandates, textbook objectives, and the desire to please others that you forget what brought you to the classroom in the first place. Infuse your teaching with your unique passions and personality—that's what will make you a teacher the students will always remember and what will help inspire your students to follow your lead, embracing life and becoming true learners. It can also encourage you to keep pursuing outside interests, nurturing the kind of inner balance that will help to fend off teacher burnout.

3. Interview the school. When you are trying to land a job, you'll be trying to make a good first impression, but keep in mind that you have a right to ask questions, too, and you *should* ask questions to make sure that you are starting out at a place that will offer you the professional scaffolding you need as a new teacher. Some questions you might ask are, "What does your school do specifically to support professional development?" "What are the class sizes, and how have they fluctuated?" "Can you tell me a little bit more about the student population and the level of parent involvement?" A good principal will appreciate a few sincere inquiries and will not become defensive. Visit the school's website and online resources before the interview to acquire a general sense of the academic focus and the particulars of the population. Exploring classroom websites created by teachers within the building will reveal a lot about the energy of the people who work there, whether teacher collaboration and parent communication are priorities, and what sort of technology and other resources might be available to you if you join the team.

Although you may not have much experience, try to do something to stand out during the interview. Work toward as many specialties or endorsements as possible on your teaching certificate. Print your résumé on attractive paper, and feel free to add a photo. If you had a formal student-teaching experience or worked with children in another setting, share a scrapbook that features snazzy bulletin boards, smiling children's faces, thank-you notes from parents, and work samples from children. Dress professionally, but if you add a pin or earrings or a tie in a cheerful color, some small, distinctive touch that shows you can be creative and fun, your potential employer will have an easier time remembering you ("the one with the bumblebee pin who brought in that photo album"). Most of all, don't take it too personally if you aren't hired right away. Teaching is very competitive, and there are plenty of behind-the-scenes or political reasons why one person is offered a position instead of another. A lot of hiring happens in a rush right before school opens, too, so don't give up hope.

4. Make a time capsule of your intentions. As a teacher you will become intimately acquainted with the required curriculum. Before you become entrenched in these requirements, find a notebook and keep a running list of what you are *excited* to teach, topics and concepts that you personally feel will be important or fun. From my own list: *Shadows and light. Letter-writing. Harlem Renaissance. Counting money. Difference between fact and opinion. Greek mythology. Solar system. Garden in an old bathtub. Sign language. Practicing handwriting to classical music. Classroom museum.* I also created a long list of books and movies, quotations, general statements and reminders to my "future self": "Teach children to set their own standards." "Sometimes the worst behavior can signal a potential within the child." "Do they know how to answer the telephone politely?" The book can be very loose. You can draw sketches of what your fantasy classroom looks like, or staple in swatches of color that would be nice for walls or curtains. You don't have to fill in all the pages. It's not an assignment; it's a mental collection of the pieces of your professional dream, a pedagogical hope chest. You may not be able to implement every idea or theme you have written (or at least not all in your first year of teaching), but you may be surprised by how much of what you want to teach may actually be part of what you are *supposed* to teach, or can be creatively integrated into the goals of the general curriculum. Being acquainted with the performance of professional athletes, for instance, may not be a mandate in the curriculum, but it is easy to incorporate into math lessons (probability, percentages, statistics), so if you enjoy talking to kids about sports, write down sports in your notebook. Likewise, children can read lyrics for sight word vocabulary, so if you're a music buff, in it goes!

This little book may become golden to you. You can look at it if you lose track of why you decided to become a teacher, or when you feel that what you have to share has been shanghaied by imposed priorities. You can find inspiration when you are determining what to do next. Looking over your ideas as a whole, you will find indicators of which grade levels you would probably be best suited to teach (finger painting, weather: primary grades; world history, web page design: older kids) and the book will guide you in gathering materials as you prepare your classroom.

Why would you do this, knowing there are so many things that are already expected of you? The agendas you set have an immediacy that contributes meaningfully to what children need to succeed, sometimes at least as much as guidelines from the state and district. Manners, for instance, may not be a major part of what you are expected to teach academically but may be a glaring part of what you determine would prepare your class for the future. Drama may be a minor part of the curriculum, but you may not want fear of public speaking to stand in the way of the children's success. You may see the national increase in childhood obesity evidenced in your room and decide to integrate more movement or nutrition studies into your day. You know that children need to know more about environmental science and media literacy than other generations may have been taught. You will want to capitalize on "teachable moments," borne from the organic interests and questions of the children. *Your* class, *your* children. Own that idea, and take personal responsibility for the children's being better off when they leave you than when they arrived, for imparting what you know to be useful and beautiful and healthy. Then you will always teach from your heart, not just tick things off of a list that someone else has given to you.

5. Build an organized collection of strategies, units, and ideas. As you come across articles, lesson plans, management techniques, or other inspiration, put them in file folders labeled thematically and organized alphabetically. These files should cover a variety of topics: Open house. Groundhog Day. Classroom management. Special needs strategies. Bulletin boards. Fishy fun. The Colonies. The Aztecs. Place value. Science experiments. Reptiles. Poetry. Martin Luther King. Astronomy. Absolutely anything that might possibly be useful in the future should go into a file, and the collection should be kept in easy reach. You can find information to fill your files by subscribing to professional magazines (a few solid picks are *Instructor, Learning, Mailbox,* and *Teacher*) and exploring well-established online teacher communities such as Educator World, Teachers .net, Teachers Helping Teachers, Teaching Tolerance, and Teaching Is a Work of Heart. Additionally, you can use the Internet to look at other teachers' classroom home pages, which will give you great ideas on topics such as decorating your classroom and communicating with parents. Your head will spin with all of the lesson plans, units, helpful hints, and general support available online, shared and created by teachers. Organizing these ideas out of the gate will make a huge difference in your efficiency in finding, using, and sharing all of these marvelous materials.

6. Read aloud to the children in your charge every single day, regardless of age or grade level. There's a lot on every teacher's plate and only so many hours in a day, and some educators feel they just don't have the time for reading to students. Others may find it awkward, reading aloud to children who are old enough to read to themselves. Cast these fallacies and fears away! In a world of educational theories, read-aloud is a fact, the proven way to guarantee a forward academic trajectory. The benefits of the practice, well documented in Jim Trelease's *Read-Aloud Handbook,* suggest that we don't have the time *not* to do it. The recommended minimum is twenty minutes, but why be chintzy? For older children, having multiple copies of a book so they can follow along while you read increases their exposure to print and allows them to absorb the mechanics and nuances of language and story instead of stressing over the task of decoding. Gathering your class together to enjoy a book at a consistent time in a cozy environment creates a community of readers and instills listening and comprehension skills that will impact every other area of the curriculum. The best reason of all to read aloud, though, is that sharing a book that you love just feels wonderful, and you deserve to feel wonderful every day. Turn on a special lamp, gather everyone around . . . Once you start this ritual, I promise, you'll be looking forward to it at least as much as the children will.

A child's confidence and ability to read directly affects academic performance and opportunity. The more you know about children's books, the more you will be able to individualize instruction and integrate reading across subject areas. With thousands of children's books released every year and thousands more published in years past, it's a challenge to navigate all of the material available in order to find those that would have the greatest positive impact. My book *How to Get Your Child to Love Reading* will make you an expert in children's literature, and my website, www.PlanetEsme.com, will direct you to my blog and others in the joyful "kidlitosphere" community that regularly review and celebrate children's books. Professional magazines like *LibrarySparks* (even if you're not a librarian), *Bookbag,* and *Book Links* offer more ideas on what books to add to your collection and how to bring books to life in a classroom context.

While you are learning about the latest and the greatest in children's literature, you can start rounding up books. This is important. You should not assume that you will be entering an environment rich with print or that the school will offer you the economic resources to develop your collection. Plus, you want a library that belongs to you and that can follow you if you change positions in the future. You can build a decent collection without too much investment through book clubs, garage sales, used bookstores, and library book sales. I and other teachers I have known have worked part time at bookstores, which offered the extra income and employee discounts that allowed us to add to our classroom libraries. Participating in national conferences such as Book Expo America (BEA), the International Reading Association (IRA), the American Library Association (ALA), the National Association for the Education for Young Children (NAEYC), as well as state and regional reading and library association conferences are often good sources of free material and informative, topical sessions. Conferences can be expensive, but even if you can only afford a pass to the exhibition hall, you'll come away with tons of catalogs, advance reader's copies, great posters, and probably a few new friends.

You can start creating a book collection before you even know what grade level you'll be teaching, and the more you learn about children's literature, the more the titles you discover can be useful regardless of the age of the children. Picture books are often stigmatized as "baby books," when in fact they contain story structure, figurative language, dialogue, character development—all of the literary elements the children should be acquainted with—in an accessible format for all levels of learners. Children are growing up in an increasingly visual world, and picture books help support the level of visual literacy that the next generation will require, so don't be afraid to use them, read them aloud, show them off, model reading them yourself, and introduce them to older kids who still need and enjoy what picture books have to offer. Conversely, children also listen at a higher "level" than they read themselves, so you can read aloud chapter books even to young kids (though you should always, always read the book through yourself to make sure the themes and treatment are age-appropriate). If you look for well-written books that inspire possibility, books that make children laugh, books in which children can recognize themselves and feel less alone, you will have a collection that will be useful across the grade levels. If you are still overwhelmed, start with a specific genre within children's literature. Picture book biographies and poetry are types of books that you will be able to read aloud and use, no matter which grade level you teach.

Finally, if you take the time to protect your investments by using fold-on covers for your hardcover slipcovers (I use the twelve-inch Fold-On Book Jacket Cover on rolls from Brodart.com, which fits most books), and clear contact paper on all the paperbacks, you'll be amazed by the difference it makes. Most damage to books happens when they are shoved into backpacks or get wet. Insist that children include a Ziploc gallon-size bag in their school supplies (if you are concerned about a choking hazard, young children can use a pillowcase instead). Any book that is borrowed from your classroom should go into a bag with the borrower's name.

7. Supplement your coursework. A lot of what a teacher-in-training reads is assigned or from a textbook. Most professors worth their salt try to assign meaningful content, but with an unprecedented number of professional resources available and teachers training in many different areas of focus and expertise, a professor can only go so far. Independently seek out alliances and mentors in print (and put a magazine rack in your bathroom so you will have time to read books of your own choosing!). Titles like *The First-Year Teacher's Survival Kit* by Julia G. Thompson, *The First Days of School* by Harry K. Wong and Rosemary T. Wong, *Discipline Without Stress, Punishment or Rewards* by Marvin L. Marshall, *The Book Whisperer* by Donalyn Miller, *What Do You Do with a Child Like This?* by L. Tobin, and *Teaching Outside the Box: How to Grab Your Students by Their Brains* by LouAnne Johnson, as well as works by authors and practitioners like Regie Routman, Madeline Hunter, John Holt, and David Elkind have the potential to inform and transform your practice on a day-to-day basis.

Take at least one extra methods class or workshop in the subject area that you feel least confident or enthusiastic about. While this initially may make you feel like groaning, it will put you in the same position that so many children are in every day: lacking in confidence but with the potential to learn. If you dedicate yourself to the idea of relearning a subject, you'll be surprised at the different perspective you enjoy. This is a powerful exercise because it's about breaking a cycle, and it's also about your own willingness to continue to learn. Visit the Bureau of Education and Research (ber.org) for dynamic speakers and workshops in your area, many of which will address areas in which you want to improve.

Consider giving attention to less obvious teaching skills, like public speaking and handwriting. Though many teachers have confidence in front of kids, some tend to buckle when other adults are around. You will have to communicate both orally and in writing with fellow teachers, parents, administrators, and other visitors on a regular basis, so strive to master your smaller bugaboos, and you can be fearless enough to teach with your door open, with limited distraction and stress.

Finally, whatever your area of study, be sure to get some special education and bilingual education experience, coursework, or training under your belt. *Every* public school teacher is a bilingual and special educator at some juncture. Prepare for those situations.

8. Find a mentor. In the course of teacher training, hopefully, you will encounter professionals who will take you under their wing, serving as advisers and allies. Their guidance and support is worth its weight in platinum.

When you begin your first year of teaching, ideally you will be formally paired with a mentor in the building, however, if this is not the case, seek one independently. As a new teacher, you will have a lot of energy, optimism, and new information to bring to the table, but even the best student of education has a lot to learn on the job. The demands of the day will put you at risk for becoming overwhelmed and isolated. Besides having a handle on subject-area content and management techniques, mentors are invaluable for reminding us not to reinvent the wheel, to take time for ourselves. They can be wellsprings of information on how to be more efficient, how to handle sticky political situations, and who in the building has a long-reach stapler. Most seasoned teachers are delighted to "pay it forward" and give you the benefit of their time, advice, and expertise. You can reciprocate by sharing new ideas and offering respect and appreciation for their insights, even when you don't agree with their approaches. If for some reason you are having difficulty finding a mentor in your school building, you can visit the well-established Mentor Center at Teachers.net and connect with a community of experienced teachers online. You don't have to take every suggestion your mentor prescribes. Independent trials and outcomes are vital to your own professional growth, so a good mentor will not try to bully you into a "right" way but lead you to it organically. My own mentor, Ismene, asked with a glint in her eye after observing me struggle through a particularly hard day, "Well? Did I give you enough rope to hang yourself?"

Another more remote but equally inspiring mentor can be a personal hero, maybe someone from history, a friend or family member, maybe somebody you have never met before but who embodies some characteristic you would like to emulate. Put up a picture or symbol of this person to remind you to aspire to that attribute. I had a glossy photo of the movie star Ann Miller in my cloakroom because she had an infectious smile and the press never caught her without it. Looking at the picture when I came in every morning reminded me to smile when I greeted the children. Another one of my heroes is Johnny Appleseed, because he planted a small seed every day and by doing so, he changed the landscape of the nation. I keep a decorative apple blossom sprig on my desk, and whenever I see it, I am reminded to read aloud, because I know it's the one seed I can plant every day that will change the landscape of the nation. These famous figures regularly impacted the way I taught. Mentors, heroes, and various angels are all around us. Strive to receive them in your teaching life.

9. Protect the children's health. School is a petri dish, and it does take some time for new teachers to build resistance to the myriad of diseases that float around the building.

Plan at least three days of general lesson plans and gather a box of extra materials in case you are absent (a fun storybook, a video, some review lessons, learning games, worksheets), as well as a seating chart, general rules, and an attendance book, clearly marked and easy to locate for the substitute teacher. In the event of illness, you won't have to drag yourself in to deal with "housekeeping."

A marked difference in the frequency of illness you experience can be made simply by washing hands regularly and insisting that children wash their hands before eating lunch and after they use the washroom. Vigilance here really does pay off. Use an antibacterial gel wash if necessary; be aware that most contain alcohol, but they're better than nothing. Don't hesitate to send a child home when he or she show signs of illness, especially a runny nose, pinkeye, or sore throat, even if the child claims to feel well; regardless of the inconvenience to parents, children do not have the right to infect you or others. Give doorknobs and keyboards an occasional swipe with an antibacterial cleansing wipe. Some teachers get on a regimen of zinc tablets, Airborne, or a gentle herbal resistance booster when they hear a child cough or sneeze. Others invest in a watercooler for the classroom, which tends to be more sanitary than a widely used school water fountain. If you express this need at an open house, maybe some generous, germ-phobic parent will ante up.

The responsibilities of a teacher to protect student health go far beyond preventing the common cold. Make sure you know how to handle an EpiPen (for severe allergic shock) and that you can recognize and help a child having an epileptic seizure or asthma attack, identify head lice and ringworm, perform an age-appropriate Heimlich maneuver, and perform age-appropriate CPR. Have a first-aid kit handy and use plastic gloves when helping a child who is bleeding or exuding other bodily fluids. Hopefully, you'll be instructed on emergency responses before the start of school, though health classes in formal teacher training programs and YMCA workshops offer this information too. Don't assume there is always a school nurse on call. Make sure you are aware of any conditions and allergies of your students, preferably even before the first day of school. Ask for this confidential information; sometimes it is not offered up.

10. Call parents with an encouraging thought or observation about their child at the start of the year. A phone call home the first week of school is one of the most valuable ways to create a bridge between home and school. Many teachers send home a letter, and while this is fine, it doesn't compare to the friendliness and accessibility of a direct conversation. You don't have to make all of the calls in one evening; spread them out over a few days.

Some parents immediately become defensive or worried about receiving a call from the teacher, which is exactly why it is imperative to make these calls. You want that first contact you make to be positive and to open lines of communication. Be quick to explain that the reason for your call is just to say hello and to introduce yourself, to say how much you are looking forward to teaching the child. Ask if there are any questions about the class or if there is any information the parent would like you to know about the child that wouldn't be in the records. Let them know about the dates and times of upcoming events (open house, assemblies, field trips, report card pickup) that they are welcome and encouraged to attend, when they should expect communication, and that if any concerns arise at any time within the school year, they should not hesitate to make an appointment with you directly. If records indicate that English is not spoken in the home, enlist a bilingual teacher's help in making the call.

Another nice by-product of phoning home is that students will likely find out that you called, which means you've got their number and aren't afraid to use it. The call suggests you're on the same team as Mama, so straighten up and fly right, but it also suggests that you are on the child's side, because you didn't call to tattle. Touch base throughout the year to celebrate a child's classroom successes, and families will more likely feel you have the child's best interests at heart and join you in a united front when necessary.

11. Start and end each day with a good word. Greet the children at the door warmly ("Good morning," "We're going to have a great day," "Glad you're back, it's not the same without you," a handshake or salute), and take them all the way to the door when they exit ("Proud of you," "Be safe going home," "You made my day fun today," slap five). This bookends the day with courtesy and goodwill.

Other kind words assure children that even if you don't like their choices, you like *them*. Remember that questions, not directives, inspire critical thinking. Try "Can you make a different choice?" instead of "Stop that." Try "How will I know this is yours?" instead of "Put your name on your paper." Try "How can we help the kids who are still trying to work?" instead of "Be quiet in the hallway." Be cognizant of the directives you keep repeating, and see if you can communicate them in a way that gives the child power and understanding over his or her behavior. Oops, I mean, can you rephrase your commands into questions and requests that require the child to take personal responsibility for actions?

12. Change your bulletin boards. You may have been in classrooms where outside the window crocuses are blooming, but inside there are still snowmen and turkeys displayed. You may have seen boards where the letters are fading, or there are shadows where old work was hung and blocked the sun, or boards that are nothing more than a messy pile of papers and announcements stapled to the wall. This is all more shabby than chic. Some folks may say, "I'm not creative, I'm not artsy," but attractive displays are very important to the mood and morale of a classroom. It makes a big difference to feel that your environment is dynamic, changing, and cheerful. If you do not believe that you are creative, you can still make sure you have seasonal store-bought bulletin board borders and accents, clean backgrounds, straight lettering, and student work on display. You can also shine transparency images onto the wall using an overhead projector and trace, enlist students to plan bulletin boards, or create a display (birthday, star student, calendar, classroom jobs, favorite book of the month) that can be changed and updated with minimal effort.

You can buy fadeless paper and ready-cut letters through teacher supply stores, though many schools have die-cut machines for cutting letters (smaller versions are also available at craft stores). You don't have to cut letters out of construction paper only; they can be cut from gift-wrapping paper, starched fabric, or newspaper. You can add dimension to your bulletin board displays by hanging items from the ceiling with fishing line or thread. You can have interactive bulletin boards in which kids lift flaps or move items from pocket to pocket on the board. Bulletin boards should always display current student work or be germane to an area currently being studied. When someone walks into your room, he or she should be able to see what your class is studying, whether or not it's "open house."

You can also "make pretty" by cleaning your blackboards daily, with a sponge and clean water and a pail (or erase your whiteboard) as part of your routine at the start or end of the day. This is the equivalent of making your bed at home. Dusty, messy blackboards are an eyesore and confuse some kids.

13. Keep moving around the classroom. Remember that your desk is for holding files and supplies, not for holding you; don't teach from behind it. You should be in constant locomotion, using your physical proximity to help guide children toward good behavioral choices, and also so that you can see who is on target and who needs help. Your back should never be to the students; and even when you're writing on the board, turn sideways frequently. Within the profession, these kind of habits are informally called "withitness," which means you have a sense of what's going on in all corners of the classroom at all times.

14. Use authentic assessments. Children's standardized test scores are not the only way to determine prior knowledge. A simple sampling at the start and end of skill-building units may prove a far more immediate and telling indicator. It will allow you to know which children have achieved your objectives even before you have begun so you can individualize instruction for children who are ready for more advanced work or recognize and offer help to those who still have deficits. You can use these samples to compare with later work to determine growth. For example, if you're going to teach long division, give the child an assignment with long division problems, without any prior instruction from you. Save and date the assignment in the student's file. At the end of several weeks of instruction and practice, present the exact same problems, and see if the child can do them. Date and save. Has the child transferred the knowledge over time? Give a similar problem again several weeks later, in a general context. Has the algorithm for long division been retained, or is more practice needed? Date and save. Another example: If you are teaching essay writing, give the child a theme on which to write without any prior instruction. After several weeks, assign the *exact same topic,* and determine whether the child has incorporated new skills. Does the child indent? Does each paragraph have a clear main idea that supports a thesis? Is there a lead sentence, a conclusion? Does the child use more thoughtful vocabulary? *What does the child know now that he or she didn't know then?* The definition of learning may be considered a change in behavior or attitude, and real changes have longevity. Bona fide learning has occurred if the child can transfer skills, that is, retain them over time to use in other appropriate situations. If a child can only perform for a single assignment or a test, the skills were not truly learned, so look for and collect evidence over a period of time.

Taking dated samples and comparing them to later work is genuinely exciting and motivating for you, the child, and the child's family to see; it's like pedagogical notches on a door frame. These kind of growth-based assessments are also helpful to show to administration if your teaching abilities are ever called into question. It's such a simple step toward accountability that so many teachers forget in the throes of all the instruction that is being delivered and amid the stresses of high-stakes testing. Take a deep breath, and add sample-gathering to the start and end of any unit.

15. Grade selectively and effectively. You don't have to put a letter or number grade on every paper. Keep a grip on what the objectives are for every assignment you give; if you end up assigning a lot of busywork, surprise, you'll have a lot of busywork, too. That's karma! Keep in mind that if you give too many practice problems without checking the work, children end up practicing the wrong way to do something. It's really important that you return papers within a few days, whether graded and commented upon or simply marked with a smile, stamp, or check mark, so the feedback is timely and meaningful. And remember, pens come in other colors besides red, and it doesn't cost anything to put a smiley face or an encouraging exclamation on a paper, though you will want to avoid exclusively telegraphing vague remarks like "good," because they aren't detailed enough to tell the child how to repeat what is "good." If you have a remark, make it is as specific as possible ("I could really see the character because you took the time to describe him," "You remembered to observe that step," "You showed your work"). Writing assignments and journaling take the longest to grade, so stagger them in a way that preserves your sanity. Establish simple rubrics, or checklists, of what you are looking for in big assignments and projects, and share them with students so they know what to include; a point system based on items on the rubric keeps grading simple for you and fair for them. Veteran teachers may be very helpful in making suggestions that streamline your organizational and time-management skills so you can finish grading and still have room for some semblance of a personal life.

16. Take baby steps toward changing student behaviors. When you encounter children who aren't good at controlling their impulses, use "successive approximations toward the goal," which is teacher talk for "you've got to crawl before you can walk." If a behavior is repetitive and disruptive, discuss it with the child, who may not even be aware of it, and create a manageable and specific goal to be met within a limited period of time ("Let's see if you can stay in your seat all through math class"). Then tape a small piece of paper with a grid on it to the child's desk; cheerful "incentive charts" are sold at teacher's supply stores, or you can make your own. For every five, ten, or fifteen minutes that the child meets the goal, go over and stamp the paper (or use a sticker or hole punch). No verbal exchange is necessary. Once the child can do it for one lesson, can he do it for two? For an hour? Half day? For the day? For a couple of days? Eventually, the charts will be abandoned, and a new behavior will be established. Be tender about setbacks; the child is likely as frustrated as you are. By starting out with reasonable goals, though, you are set up to create success and confidence about self-control in the long run.

17. Show your love through high expectations. Some children come from terrible circumstances, have holes in their prior knowledge, or struggle with Herculean learning differences. They may have lots of excuses, some very viable, for why work is unfinished or why they are otherwise behind. As a new teacher, you will naturally feel the desire to be liked by your students, and you will want to show empathy and gain their trust; making accommodations to match their explanations seems like a natural means to those ends. It is important, however, to be sensitive to these situations without being enabling; otherwise the children will begin to confuse their situation with their potential. There may be many good reasons why the world says "they can't," but as soon as *you* say "they can't," you have just punctuated the end of their pedagogical possibilities with a dreary period. Just as is the case with modifying behavior, high academic expectations doesn't mean making things hard for kids; it means setting them up to succeed by breaking tasks into manageable pieces. Once you have done your part, anticipate that with practice and diligence, they can and will meet whatever challenges stand in the way of that success.

18. Mind your behind. "CYA" is the universal teacher code for "cover your ass." You are going to get in trouble by accident at some juncture, that's the nature of the beast, but there are a few basics to keep you out of teacher stew:

- Keep your hands off the kids. This is actually not terrifically realistic, especially in the primary grades when the children gather around for hugs, but know that it is the expectation from an administrative point of view, and certainly, no corporal punishment is allowed.

- Don't ever be alone with one child. Keep your door open, and always have another adult or at least another student present. This is a good idea for all teachers but especially imperative for men, who are perpetually vulnerable to suspicion.

- Don't ever leave your class alone, even if the children are well behaved. Let the office or a teaching neighbor know if you need to be excused in an emergency. Smoking and coffee are not emergencies.

- Keep detailed, dated records of behavioral problems.

- Keep detailed, dated records of any communications with parents and administration. Carbon-duplicate notepads are available at teacher supply stores.

- Document incidences of student misbehavior and samples of work that suggest possible special needs so you can make referrals when necessary.

- Stick to individual educational plans that have been established for children with learning, emotional, or behavioral problems and differences.

- Keep parents apprised of the child's progress, and attempt to make contact if there are any precipitous changes; there should be no surprises at report card pickup.

- Report suspected child abuse and neglect to administration (preferably in writing) and to the appropriate state agency.

- Keep an accurate attendance book and grade book, and an up-to-date lesson plan book. Keep student records confidential.

- Keep student safety paramount. You should know where your students are at all times.

- Don't smoke or drink at school, and don't buy drugs from the seventh graders.

- Don't interrupt instruction to conduct personal calls on your cell phone.

- Post emergency procedures where they can be easily seen.

- Have a union representative present when you anticipate a serious conversation with administration, and have administration present when you anticipate a serious conversation with parents.

- Try to de-escalate problems directly with co-workers before complaining to administration, and don't say anything behind the back of anyone in the building that you wouldn't be willing to say to his or her face. Duplicity, gossip, and tattling will invariably bite you in the behind. As one principal I worked for sagely advised the staff about verbal unkindness: "You'll have an easier time getting toothpaste back in the tube than you will have putting words back in your mouth."

- Children usually think teachers are playing favorites; don't give them any legitimate reasons to believe it.

- On field trips, bring back the same number of children that you took. Preferably from the same school.

- Last but not least, if you insist upon making up funny names for yourself and then ask the children to refer to you that way, you might find yourself in some hot water. So bring the bubble bath.

There, that should do it. Shouldn't it? *Shouldn't* it?

19. Make school an oasis. It's helpful for teachers to know when children have had a death or illness in the family, when there is a divorce, when living situations change drastically, or when there are environments of abuse or poverty. These impact learning. But be aware that it is sometimes an especially loving thing to let children come to school and escape difficulties they experience at home. You don't have any say-so over when Daddy gets paroled, and Mommy's drinking problem isn't something a teacher's influence usually can sway. Keep hold of the bigger picture, and encourage the children to do the same. If children are perpetually reminded of difficulties at home while at school, they can lose focus and self-esteem, and then they may fail to gain the skills they need to live a different sort of life when they grow up. Sometimes new teachers become caught up in the drama of a child's life, but they must be careful not to overreach, imagining that their concern is in any way a substitute for counseling and services that a family may need. If you know a child is having serious problems, offer to be a listening ear, research and offer resources to the family, and report to authorities as the law may require. Don't ever underestimate the power of simply giving a child a nice day to look forward to as both a great temporary salve and a contribution to a long-term cure.

20. Say "I don't know." As a self-contained classroom teacher, you may teach more than half a dozen subjects, and it is very unlikely that anyone would be masterful at all of them. When you can't model being an expert, model being a learner. When a child asks a question that you don't know the answer to, admit that you don't know or that you aren't sure, and model the process of finding out. Whip out a dictionary, look something up online, or ask for help from others (including students). If it is not something you can address at that moment, write the question down and make a point of getting back to the child, sharing how you found the information as well as the answer.

"I don't know" is also a healthy response in professional situations. Though as a new teacher you are eager to show your proficiency, there can be professionalism in admitting when you need help to get the job done. Ask experienced teachers how to perform tasks correctly and efficiently. In meetings and in exchanges with administration, it is also all right and prudent to say, "I don't know," and "I'm not sure," and ask if you can give the issue a little more thought. This may go against your personality; teachers tend to want to give the right answer, to be the ones who know. The old adage says, "The wisest man is one who knows there is much he does not know." True dat.

21. Be consistent. Any fantasy you may have about a successful teaching experience is invisibly anchored to classroom management skills. The best behaviors you may have observed, such as children seeming to know what to do without much direction, or children listening respectfully to you and to each other, or children fully engaged in an activity to the point that they lose track of time or don't want it to end, all have been hard-won by the teacher at some point by virtue of experience and consistency. Consistency is the holy grail of classroom management. It means you do what you say and you say what you mean, you mean the same thing on Tuesday as you do on Thursday, and you mean the same thing for Johnny as you do for Janey. It means you are fair and constant and that people around you know what to expect. It means, "This is the way we do things around here." Sometimes adults think that consistency limits children's freedom and creativity, but consistency isn't synonymous with inflexibility. Rather, you are not renegotiating the rules and procedures to the point that it impedes your ability to make the most of the time that you share together. It can actually afford more time for creativity and concentration on tasks that you and the children deem important.

You can start by articulating rules, procedures, and consequences early on. In fact, these should be well established and communicated by the end of the first week. The trick is sticking to them! Sometimes teachers don't follow up with a consequence or they let children explain extenuating circumstances at length in an effort to be nice or fair. Well, there is nothing nice about it, because, in fact, what you have said to a child is, "When I say something, I don't mean it; it all depends on my mood and how fast you can talk." In which case, everything you say afterward will be suspect. For example, if you suggest that you are going to make things better for them, or that they are intelligent, or that they are not in danger, this, too, may be suspect, and children may resort to defense mechanisms to protect themselves. Inconsistent teachers make for very scary classrooms, and I mean that quite literally. Children have to be able to believe everything you say in order to feel safe.

At some point every teacher feels the loathing that comes from having to deliver a consequence that was promised but that he or she doesn't really want to deliver. You may have established "No recess, if . . ." and then, after they test those limits, you are stuck with them in the classroom all recess when you needed that break to do something else. You may have been looking forward to a classroom party or a field trip even more than they have. With experience, you will learn to say only what you mean, toning the extremity of your "if/then" statements down a few notches. You will learn to take a breath even in the heat of the moment and look a few steps ahead. There may also be occasions when you realize that, for whatever reason, you have gone overboard, in which case you can apologize and temper a consequence to be more reasonable. If you've been consistent all along, this should feel like a governor's reprieve, rare enough to elicit gratefulness from the children, but not an expectation.

Over the years, I have found that three simple classroom rules cover all the bases: "looking" (at the person whose turn it is to speak), "listening" (to the teacher or whoever has been called on to speak), and "consideration" (which means we go out of our way not to drive each other crazy). When you ask children to make up rules, they usually start with "don't" statements, because they hear a lot of "don'ts," and it's so exciting to be able to say "don't" to someone else for a change that they can hardly contain themselves. "Don't chew gum." (This falls under consideration.) "No talking." (This falls under listening.) "Don't kick your neighbor's chair." (Consideration again.) A lot of teacher-training programs advise that children be part of creating classroom rules, that it makes them more invested. While I see the rationale in this approach, in practice I haven't seen that much difference in the investment. If you are in the role of delivering consequences, especially as a new teacher, it is very important that *you* are invested in the rules so you are more likely to be consistent. If you want to include children in the process of developing boundaries, a more meaningful conversation to have with children has to do with rights and responsibilities. As a teacher, you have the right to change seating arrangements. You have the right to give directions without having to talk over other people's voices. Students have the right to know what's coming next in their day, to be included in games on the playground, to make up work when they have been sick, to be able to hear what the teacher is saying. Rights and responsibilities are an ongoing conversation. I think kids, like adults, just want to know what's allowed and what's not, and to feel that the boundaries are reasonable.

The challenges of classroom management have delivered a knock-out punch to many a well-meaning new teacher, but if you can stay in the ring, in time you will not rely on the excessive negative consequences that are the mark of a reactionary novice trying to manage a large or unruly group. Instead, you will become expert at setting a climate of expectation and camaraderie that is livable and humane, delivering on the promise of positive outcomes for positive behaviors, operating on students' intrinsic motivations, and creating consensus or group meetings to solve problems. In the long run, as a consistent teacher, you'll find yourself held in esteem not because the kids were able to control you but because you helped them to control themselves.

22. Hone in on homework. Be judicious about the kind of homework you assign so that children are not ultimately assessed on family support over which they have no control. Many children live with adults who are functionally illiterate or innumerate, and this is true across socioeconomic strata. Children may live in crowded apartments where it is difficult to find a quiet space. They may have parents who are working two jobs or parents who are negligent or self-involved; in either case a child might be left with impressive responsibilities for household chores or sibling caretaking. Many children have been identified as students with special needs and have IEPs (Individualized Education Plans) on file, which suggest modified approaches to learning that must be accommodated by law. With these kinds of factors in mind, the only homework you should be assigning is independent reading (books on tape are available for students with special needs), completion of work that was explained and started at school (this should always be practice of a concept taught at school; new concepts should *never* be introduced in the context of homework), and projects for which you are certain they have the necessary supplies.

23. Strive to increase your engaged time. Engaged time is the time a child spends on-task, working toward objectives you have set. If you were to time your day, or even a single lesson, you might be chagrined to discover the shockingly large chunk that gets lost to transitioning from subject to subject or room to room, taking out materials, taking roll or collecting work, organizing groups, addressing minor discipline problems and conflicts, handling unanticipated interruptions from other adults, and simply veering off track with a little pleasant conversational detour from the lesson plan. If you were to lose even a half hour of engaged time from a five-hour school day (not including lunch and recess), in a week, you would have lost almost a half day of school. That's two days a month, or sixteen days of school a year. That's a two-week vacation going on while you're at work! Hours engaged in your classroom will positively correlate to the ultimate academic success of the children you serve, in both testing and practice, so tighten your time line with a few simple tips:

- Have meaningful review or practice work posted when the children enter the room, or use the time for independent reading.

- Children should be doing their own work while you take attendance and lunch count.

- Post your schedule, and hold to it as best you can.

- Start each lesson with an "anticipatory set," that is, a lively activity or explanation that allows the students to "change gears" and lets their brains know, "Oh, we are working on *this* now."

- Make transitions snappier by establishing procedures so kids know what they are expected to do (line up, take out materials, pass papers forward, leave homework in the mailbox) and how they are supposed to do it. Use consistent sensory-based signals (clapping, lights, kazoo!) to let children know when it's time to move on or begin a new activity.

- Children should know how to leave to use the washroom without interrupting the class to ask your permission (some students let teachers know when they have to go by raising two fingers or some other quiet signal).

- Children should know what work to do or what activities are available to them if they finish assignments early.

- Compile assignments for absent students so you don't have to hunt for the work upon their return.

- Deliver and pick up students punctually from activities that take place outside of your classroom.

- Intersperse the day with periods of movement, interaction with nature and each other, and as much fresh air as possible so the children can be more attentive when it's time to sit still.

- Boredom = management problems, and management problems = a time drain. Keep children engaged by easing up on worksheets. Instead, give them projects that tap into a variety of brain modalities (or "multiple intelligences," as described by Dr. Howard Gardner: logic smart, body smart, music smart, nature smart, people smart, picture smart, self smart, and word smart), or allow them to synthesize different skills at once. Time flies when kids have a hands-on project . . . and most of it is time on task!

- Have a set time and strategy (like a conflict resolution model) for dealing with issues that arise as a classroom community, and do not entertain every little complaint before then.

- Ignore, ignore, ignore. Do not interrupt your own instruction to stop someone from kicking a chair leg or passing notes or staring out into space. Use your physical proximity to cue the child to make a different choice, or talk to the child after class.

24. Stop beating yourself up. As a teacher, you may do a hundred good and decent and helpful things a day, but one mistake will keep you up all night. It's easy to feel monstrous; you are in a position of great power, but you are also a human being who may be tired, hormonal, or struggling with complicated personal situations. You will occasionally lose your cool, slip with the wrong word, or a word spoken maybe just a little too loudly or unkindly. Maybe your instructional style will fail to scintillate. Maybe you'll forget something important, maybe you'll put your foot in your mouth with a colleague. As you probably say to the kids: Tomorrow is a new day. A chance to say, "I'm sorry," a chance to do better. In most cases, the classroom is a place of fast healing; children are forgiving and resilient and grow two inches for every genuine bit of encouragement you impart. Most likely, you haven't done half the damage you imagine. Even if you did, be fortified by knowing that on other days you are giving the children enough skills that someday they should be able to afford a good psychiatrist.

Speaking of which: The demands of the profession are behemoth and as a result teachers are prone to depression, exhaustion, marital problems, and stress. A well-known quote by educational consultant Neila Connors warns, "If you don't feed the teachers, they eat the students." Teaching is the sort of job that you could easily do 24/7 and still not feel caught up, so at some point you will have to make a conscious decision to put reasonable limits on the hours you spend on work. Prepare in advance: buy nonrefundable tickets to a show or sports event, or sign up for a class. Gift wrap bath beads, chocolates, a new CD or DVD or book, a gift certificate for a massage or manicure, the phone number of a nonteaching friend you wish you could talk to more often, to unwrap "in case of emergency." Keep photos of family, pets, and loved ones around to remind you of your priorities. Try to support your intimate relationships by making a special date that you keep religiously with a spouse or best friend every four to six weeks. Let your wider circle of friends know that you may be a bit remote for a while, but assure them (and yourself) that it's par for the course for being a first-year teacher. Try hard to do something for yourself, even if only for a few minutes every day, that is not directly related to teaching: sing a song, meditate or work out, craft, cook, garden, watch the news. If you maintain an outside life and keep in touch with the popular culture, you'll have so much more to offer inside the school.

If you find yourself crying, yelling, or having violent outbursts with any regularity, or you start to abuse substances in order to deal with your job, seek out a professional counselor; also find a discreet veteran in the profession to advise you, because a therapist won't necessarily be acquainted with the pragmatic logistical measures that can make such a huge difference in your day-to-day sense of sanity. Find solace in the fact that while other years may be difficult, there is really nothing quite like the first year, and everything you learn the hard way now you can do an easier way later. Meanwhile, recharge your "mojo" with positive and affirming self-talk, such as:

Teaching is such important, worthwhile work.
I want to be a teacher.
I have so much to share.
I have patience, knowledge, and kindness inside of me.
I make a difference in the lives of the children. The children make a difference in my life.
It's okay to ask for help.
It's okay to make mistakes.
If I am tired, I will find the time to rest.
If I take time for myself, I will be a better teacher.

25. Keep a diary. The first year in a classroom of your own is an epic adventure. According to Ellen Moir of the New Teacher Center, there are five phases of first-year teaching: anticipation, survival, disillusionment, rejuvenation, and reflection. Jotting down your experiences even once in a while will help you to recognize your place in this trajectory, and it's great therapy to boot. Journaling will help you to feel less alone, to revel privately in your achievements, large and small; and it will allow you to see the difference you might have made without even realizing it. Journaling will allow you to think about the people you work with, for, and against and help you examine your role in these relationships—and consider what you really want from others, from yourself, and from your life. Most of all, a diary will help you to remember. Take a photo of your inner self, for you will not always be the teacher you are now. Like the children, you are going to grow and change. And who knows? Maybe someone else will read your diary and embark on an adventure of his or her own.

There are actually two shopping lists you need for the first day of school. One of them goes home with the children and may include these basic items:

Pencils

Pens

Folders with pockets

Composition notebook

Glue (stick and/or bottle)

Crayons, markers, colored pencils

Ruler

Scissors

Index cards

Ream of copy paper

Ream of notebook paper

Box of Kleenex

Roll of paper towels

Be aware that some households may need the supply list in another language. Avoid insisting on expensive brand names. Make sure to have a set of supplies for children whose guardians do not come through, or have all supplies go into a community collection to be shared as needed. Let families know that at some point in the school year you will be reissuing a supply list for consumables (things that get used up and need to be replenished, like pencils, pens, art supplies, and paper products).

As for your own supplies, here are some basics for your pantry, desk, classroom environment, and wish list:

❏ Adhesive address labels (with name and room number to mark personal belongings)
❏ Air purifier/humidifier
❏ Airborne or zinc tablets
❏ Aluminum foil
❏ Aspirin or other pain reliever
❏ Baby wipes (great for quickly cleaning off glue and paint from hands)
❏ Board games, card games, and puzzles for indoor recess (ask parents for gently used items)
❏ Book covers
❏ Breath mints
❏ Broom and dustpan
❏ Bulletin board alphabet (in print or cursive)
❏ Bulletin board borders
❏ Bulletin board letters
❏ Bulletin board background paper

NEW TEACHER SHOPPING LIST

- ❏ Calculator
- ❏ Calendar for the class
- ❏ Camera
- ❏ CD or tape player
- ❏ Chalk and eraser
- ❏ Change of clothes for a child, in whatever general size suits your grade level (get a T-shirt and drawstring sweatpants at the Goodwill—accidents happen)
- ❏ Children's books, bookshelves, and displays
- ❏ Clear contact paper
- ❏ Curtains
- ❏ Dental floss
- ❏ Dry-erase markers
- ❏ Dustbuster
- ❏ Easel and paper
- ❏ Electric pencil sharpener
- ❏ Envelopes (regular and manila)
- ❏ Fans (if your school is not air-conditioned)
- ❏ File cabinet and files
- ❏ First-aid kit, rubber gloves, cute band-aids
- ❏ Flag
- ❏ Flashlight
- ❏ Glass/wood cleaner

NEW TEACHER SHOPPING LIST

- ☐ Glitter
- ☐ Glue (stick and bottle)
- ☐ Grade book
- ☐ Hand bell or whistle
- ☐ Hand sanitizer
- ☐ Hanging map
- ☐ Happy box (fill with rewards like stickers, bookmarks, pencils)
- ☐ In-box/out-box
- ☐ Index cards
- ☐ Lamp
- ☐ Large dictionary and thesaurus
- ☐ Lesson plan book
- ☐ Library pockets
- ☐ Long-reach and regular stapler, staple remover
- ☐ Loose change (bring in your penny jar; you'll use it at lunch count)
- ☐ Loose-leaf rings
- ☐ Mailboxes
- ☐ Magnet (great for picking up spilled paper clips, staples, and thumbtacks)
- ☐ Markers (colored, dry-erase, permanent)
- ☐ Maxi pads (men, if you teach girls in the fourth grade

and up, keep a few, too; hand very discreetly in paper if requested or necessary)

- ❏ Microwave popcorn (it will make you popular at teacher's meetings)
- ❏ Nameplates (desks, locker, cubby, and one fancy one for you, teacher!)
- ❏ Needle, thread, and safety pins
- ❏ One-hole and three-hole paper punches
- ❏ Pail and sponge
- ❏ Paper (construction, lined and copy/printer, scratch)
- ❏ Paper clips, bulldog clips, paper fasteners
- ❏ Paper cups, plates, napkins
- ❏ Personal appointment calendar
- ❏ Plants
- ❏ Pocket chart
- ❏ Poster board
- ❏ Post-it notes
- ❏ Printer ink
- ❏ Rubber bands
- ❏ Rubber stamps and inkpads (my favorites at kidstamps.com)
- ❏ Rug
- ❏ Ruler and yardstick

NEW TEACHER SHOPPING LIST

- ❏ Stepladder
- ❏ Stickers
- ❏ Storage boxes
- ❏ Storytelling chair
- ❏ Tape (clear, packing, and masking)
- ❏ Timer
- ❏ Thank-you notes
- ❏ Thinking cap
- ❏ Throat lozenges
- ❏ Thumbtacks
- ❏ Trouble basket
- ❏ Vase
- ❏ Wall mount tabs
- ❏ Watercooler
- ❏ Zip drive
- ❏ Ziploc bags (sandwich, quart, gallon size)

Is *that* all? This list does not include subject-specific materials, like those you can use for arts and crafts (such as
tempera paints, yarn, clay, brown paper bags, craft sticks,
feathers, googly eyes, pipe cleaners, paper plates, colored
tissue paper), math and science (baking soda, measurement sets, thermometers, scales, a microscope, magnets,
models, Cuisenaire rods, counters, play money, calculators,

compasses), early childhood education (sand table, puppets, blocks, flannelboard, rhythm instruments, dress-up clothes), social studies (newspapers, time machine), reading materials (multiple-copy sets, magazines), or general hardware (computer, overhead projector and transparencies, paper cutter, dry erase boards, laminator, VCR and monitor, listening center).

When you land your first teaching assignment, scope out which supplies are already available to you in a general supply locker, teacher's lounge, or your classroom, and fill in the gaps as you are able. Teachers subsidize school systems; it is not uncommon for a new teacher to spend hundreds, sometimes thousands of dollars out of pocket. This burden tends to abate somewhat as time goes on and materials are accumulated. One of the great challenges of being an educator is learning to work with what you have and realizing your vision of a classroom within your financial means. While this may be frustrating at times, no need to despair; many great minds have come forth from schoolrooms with much less than we have today. Luckily, the most important supplies you bring to the room can't be bought at any store: they are your inventiveness, your resiliency and dedication, your resourcefulness, your empathy for the children, your example, and the time you have spent in preparation for your momentous first day, a day that you can reinvent every September.

Good luck!

Esmé Raji Codell

"One of the nation's most sought-after voices for empowering teachers" (*People* magazine), a "superstar of education" (*Scholastic Instructor*), and "the first lady of read-aloud" (*Teaching K-8 Magazine*), Esmé Raji Codell is an educator with many years of experience in the Chicago Public Schools and beyond. *Educating Esmé* won *ForeWord Magazine*'s memoir of the year and first place for national education reporting from the Education Writers Association. Her novels for children have received numerous awards as well. A nationally renowned children's literature specialist and the author of *How to Get Your Child to Love Reading,* she was the recipient of a prestigious Patterson PageTurner Award for spreading the excitement of books in an effective and original way. As an advocate for literacy and literature-based instruction, Esmé has been a featured speaker at the National Museum for Women in the Arts and has appeared on CBS's *The Early Show* and CNN. Her performance prowess was also seen on C-SPAN's *Booknotes* and heard on NPR's *Voice of America.* She has been a keynote speaker for the International Reading Association, the Society of Children's Book Writers and Illustrators, and the American Library Association. Esmé lives with her husband and son in Chicago, where she runs the popular children's literature website PlanetEsme.com, and the unique literary salon the PlanetEsmé Bookroom, "Chicago's Literary Living Room." Esmé is available for select speaking engagements. Please contact speakersbureau@workman.com.

Other Books on Education from Algonquin

The Children in Room E4: American Education on Trial, by Susan Eaton

"*The Children in Room E4* is a wonderful, complex, subtle, and intelligent work that digs deep into the crisis facing urban education. The long legal battles that surround the notorious racial segregation of one city are set against an intimate narrative of life within one classroom and the struggles and achievements of one teacher and her students. The narrative itself is utterly compelling, but it is the political context of this story that lends it national significance. A very important book. It ought to be read widely." —Jonathan Kozol, author of *The Shame of the Nation*

"A damning book that shines light on a particularly American dilemma." —*Entertainment Weekly*

EDUCATION/SOCIAL SCIENCE • ISBN-13 978-1-56512-617-6

Work Hard. Be Nice: How Two Inspired Teachers Created the Most Promising Schools in America, by Jay Mathews

"Two stories are masterfully woven together here. One is of two young men—think Tom Sawyer and Huck Finn—setting out on an adventure to teach children how to read, write, and behave in some of our toughest urban classrooms. The other story is of the children themselves, mostly poor and minority, soaring to life in their new environment . . . Jay Mathews deserves great credit for telling the tale so well—and for making a compelling case that, yes, we can change public education." —David Gergen, professor of public service and director, Center for Public Leadership, Harvard Kennedy School

EDUCATION • ISBN-13 978-1-56512-516-2

In Code: A Young Woman's Mathematical Journey,
by Sarah Flannery with David Flannery

"What every aspiring young scientist and mathematician needs: love, humor, inspiration and . . . a copy of this book." —Richard Mankiewicz, author of *The Story of Mathematics*

"A marvelous book . . . I recommend the book to anyone who is interested in mathematics and especially youngsters—males as well as females . . . A most remarkable book." —*Mathematics Teacher* magazine

EDUCATION/MATHEMATICS • ISBN-13 978-1-56512-377-9